The Leader's Guide to Working with Underperforming Teachers

Under increasing pressure in the face of teacher evaluation systems and accountability measures, schools must focus on those teachers who exhibit marginal to incompetent teaching behaviors in their classrooms. This book is a vital resource for educational leaders who are responsible for instructional programs and teacher evaluation. Zepeda's tried-and-true strategies will help you take the necessary steps to support and mentor struggling teachers by detecting underperformance, developing strategies to help teachers, engaging in difficult conversations to enact plans of improvement, and following legal requirements. The practical tools found in this book will help teachers improve their instruction, assessment, classroom management, and teamwork.

Sally J. Zepeda is Professor of Educational Administration and Policy at the University of Georgia, where she teaches courses in instructional supervision, professional development, teacher evaluation, and school improvement.

The Leader's Guide to Working with Underperforming Teachers

Overcoming Marginal Teaching and Getting Results

Sally J. Zepeda

Routledge
Taylor & Francis Group

NEW YORK AND LONDON

First published 2016
by Routledge
711 Third Avenue, New York, NY 10017

and by Routledge
2 Park Square, Milton Park, Abingdon, Oxon, OX14 4RN

Routledge is an imprint of the Taylor & Francis Group, an informa business

Library of Congress Cataloging in Publication Data
Names: Zepeda, Sally J., 1956– author.
Title: The leader's guide to working with underperforming teachers : overcoming marginal teaching and getting results / Sally J. Zepeda.
Description: New York, NY : Routledge, 2016. | Includes bibliographical references.
Identifiers: LCCN 2015037835| ISBN 9781138855779 (hardback) | ISBN 9781138855786 (pbk.) | ISBN 9781315720135 (ebook)
Subjects: LCSH: Teachers – Rating of. | Teacher effectiveness. | Performance standards. | Mentoring in education. | Educational leadership.
Classification: LCC LB2838 .Z47 2016 | DDC 371.14/4–dc23
LC record available at http://lccn.loc.gov/2015037835

ISBN: 978-1-138-85577-9 (hbk)
ISBN: 978-1-138-85578-6 (pbk)
ISBN: 978-1-315-72013-5 (ebk)

Typeset in Optima
by HWA Text and Data Management, London

Contents

Meet the Author

Sally J. Zepeda, Ph.D., a former K–12 administrator and teacher, is a professor at the University of Georgia in the Department of Lifelong Education, Administration, and Policy. She teaches courses related to instructional supervision, teacher and leader evaluation, and professional development.

Dr. Zepeda has published numerous articles in such journals as the *Journal of Curriculum and Supervision; Alberta Journal of Educational Research; Educational Assessment, Evaluation and Accountability; School Leadership and Management Journal; Review of Educational Research; International Journal of Mentoring and Coaching in Education; Educational Management Administration & Leadership;* and the *International Journal of Educational Management.* She has also authored, co-authored, or edited more than 25 books including *Job-Embedded Professional Development: Support, Collaboration, and Learning in Schools,* the highly acclaimed third edition of *The Principal as Instructional Leader: A Handbook for Supervisors,* the third edition of *Instructional Supervision: Applying Tools and Concepts,* and the third edition of *Informal Classroom Observations On the Go: Feedback, Discussion, and Reflection* with Routledge.

Dr. Zepeda served for 9 years as the book and audio review column editor for the *Journal of Staff Development* and as chair of the American Education Research Association Supervision SIG. She also serves on the editorial boards for several scholarly and practitioner journals, including the *International Journal of Mentoring and Coaching in Education* and the *International Journal of Teacher Leadership.* Dr. Zepeda is a member of the Council of Professors of Instructional Supervision (COPIS) and a lifetime Fellow in the Foundation for Excellence in Teaching.

In 2005, Dr. Zepeda received the inaugural Master Professor Award from the University Council of Educational Administration. Dr. Zepeda received the 2010 Russell H. Yeany, Jr., Research Award honoring outstanding contributions to research and, in 2011, the Distinguished Research Mentor Award from the University of Georgia. In 2014, Dr. Zepeda (with her co-author) was awarded the Paula Silver Case Award in the *Journal of Cases in Educational Leadership* (Best Case in 2013).

Dr. Zepeda has worked with many school systems in the United States and overseas, especially the Middle East, to support teacher and leader development. As a system-wide professor-in-residence with the Clarke County School District (Athens, GA), Dr. Zepeda assists with teacher and leader effectiveness initiatives that have included the development of a teacher and leader evaluation system, fidelity studies related to observable practices for teachers and leaders, and other projects related to professional learning for leaders since 2011.

Preface

The Approaches Running Throughout This Book

The Leader's Guide to Working with Underperforming Teachers: Overcoming Marginal Teaching and Getting Results is written for school and system leaders to approach teacher underperformance primarily in the classroom. If you supervise and evaluate teachers, then this book is for you! Each chapter examines critical areas with which leaders need to be familiar to address teacher underperformance. However, many of the strategies and concepts offered can be applied to the work a leader does with all teachers in the building.

By examining the table of contents, the reader will see that the areas within the book follow a progression that ranges *from* detecting underperformance, developing strategies to support teachers, and engaging in difficult conversations *to* enacting plans of improvement, following legal requirements and, if all else fails, compassionately and courageously pointing to the exit sign on the door. Teacher evaluation has changed dramatically in the past few years; however, the intents have remained the same—teacher effectiveness, growth, and development are the foundation for all efforts. These critical areas underscore that school leaders are responsible not only for the school program but also, more pointedly, for ensuring that every student is taught by a competent teacher.

The concepts and skills are presented to help the leader bolster instructional capacity and effective teaching and work with a teacher whose performance stalls the needle from moving forward to student growth, blemishes the instructional program, and thwarts the efforts to meet school improvement targets associated with being accountable for student learning. A brief sketch is provided as an advanced organizer for delving more deeply into areas within the chapters that target key concepts, skills, and approaches.

What's Inside the Chapters?

Chapter 1: Framing the Issues About Underperforming Teachers

The range of teacher performance is examined as are the complexities teachers and leaders experience with ratcheting accountability for student success. A brief overview of teacher quality and teacher effectiveness is offered. The chapter concludes with an examination of the new work of school leaders who must now be in a position to assess and proactively address sub-par teaching.

Chapter 2: Teacher Evaluation in a Nutshell

Teacher evaluation is fundamentally different given the focus on teacher quality, ratcheting accountability, and federal and state policies and waivers (e.g., federal Race to the Top program) that now govern these systems. The complexities of value-added measures are examined, as are the types of supervision and professional development needed to support teachers—all teachers, but especially those who are underperforming.

The Every Student Succeeds Act of 2015 (ESSA) was signed into law in December, 2015 and does not mandate teacher or leader evaluations; instead, ESSA leaves the policies related to the evaluation of teachers and leaders to the discretion of the states and removes the requirement that they use standardized test results to evaluate teachers. The shifts in power now situate states as the major decision makers in matters related to teacher and leader evaluation.

Chapter 3: Making the Commitment to Effective Teaching

The assessment of teaching is at the center of teacher evaluation systems, and this chapter examines the relationship between teacher performance standards and the instructional practices that give life to the standards and support the assessment of teaching. The chapter highlights common teacher evaluation frameworks as well as the commitment needed to ensure effective teaching in every classroom every day.

Chapter 4: Underperforming Teachers In and Out of the Classroom

Marginal performance can be detected in and out of the classroom. Cues for uncovering underperformance as well as possible causes are examined. This chapter helps to prepare the leader to respond to underperformance and then examines some possible responses from teachers once underperformance is brought to their attention.

Chapter 5: Conversations Needed to Work with Underperforming Teachers

Conversations are essential for engaging all teachers in the talk about teaching and learning. Effective leaders create the conditions for having open conversations, even the difficult ones, with teachers. This chapter outlines key strategies for preparing for difficult conversations as well as strategies to ensure that momentum for improvement is created.

Chapter 6: Improvement Planning with the Underperforming Teacher

Moving a teacher into a plan of improvement necessitates having formal conversations, creating written documentation, and ensuring key personnel and resources are available to support teachers who need to improve in the classroom. Monitoring the formal plan of improvement is essential.

Chapter 7: The Complexities Leaders Face in Working with Underperforming Teachers

Leaders who work with underperforming teachers face complexities related to new teacher evaluation systems, experience psychological stressors, and find that time on task is often diluted by the organizational patterns found in the work of leading a school. School culture is examined as a backdrop for the work principals must do while supporting underperforming teachers.

Chapter 8: Keeping Classroom Issues Out of the Courtroom: Legal Principles for Supervisors Confronting Underperforming Teachers

Such legal principles as due process, issues surrounding value-added measures, and teacher evaluation, the basics of documentation related to the plan of improvement, and movement toward non-renewal or termination are examined so as to help the leader keep key principles in mind while working with underperforming teachers.

Chapter 9: The Consequences of Doing Nothing and Making Tough Decisions When All Else Fails

Making tough decisions—namely, whether an underperforming teacher has made enough progress to (1) come off the plan of improvement, (2) extend the plan of improvement based on progress, or (3) move toward non-renewal—are examined in this chapter. The leader is led through pulling together artifacts and evidence and analyzing and looking for patterns related to teacher performance. Issues related to the fallout from decisions a leader makes are examined.

Chapter 10: Final Perspectives

The book ends by highlighting key takeaways from the chapters, focusing attention on the work of the leader.

Acknowledgments

Many people work behind the scenes when an author writes a book, and the work includes such tasks as proofing pages to ensure all references are present and searching libraries for the latest and greatest articles, chapters, and books to support the development of ideas and concepts. Atakan Ata, a research assistant and doctoral student in educational administration and policy at the University of Georgia was relentless in supporting efforts to meet deadlines. Atakan's work ethic is nothing less than spectacular. Tayler Rae Brinson also supported this effort through her eye to detail. Both Atakan and Tayler Rae pitched in so I could make the words flow.

Professor Tim Rowland (University of East Anglia, Norwich, Norfolk) provided insight and led me to the right sources at the right time to further my understandings about politeness theory and face-saving acts.

Dr. Muhammad Akram, an assistant professor at University of Education, Lahore, Pakistan, was generous with his time and efforts, leading me to resources about teacher effectiveness and self-assessment.

Dr. Ann Blankenship wrote Chapter 8 in this book, given her expertise in school law. Dr. Blankenship's contribution filled a need for an authoritative examination of the legal issues school leaders might face in working with underperforming teachers.

No book is ever complete without the thoughtful and reflective insights provided by the reviewers, whose wisdom was apparent in their critical but constructive feedback to the book prospectus. I am indebted to their goodwill and keen insights.

A very special acknowledgment goes to my colleagues in the Clarke County School District (Athens, GA) who provided counsel when translations from research and theory to practice were needed. Dr. Philip D. Lanoue, superintendent of the Clarke County School District and the 2015 American Association of School Administrators National Superintendent of the Year, openly gave of his time, shared resources, and engendered the belief that a book with recency for leaders to support underperforming teachers was needed in the field. Thanks always, Phil, for your impressive intellect and poignant feedback. Dr. Sherri Freeman, associate superintendent for human resources, was always willing to offer sage counsel when needed.

I am humbled by the many conversations over the years with Dr. Noris Price, superintendent of Baldwin County Schools, Dr. Wanda Creel, superintendent of Gainesville City School System, Dr. Selena Blankenship, principal of Hilsman Middle School, Dr. Robbie Hooker, principal of Clarke Central High School, Dr. Brad Bowling, principal of Westside Middle School, and countless other building and central office leaders who always took the time to listen to my ideas and challenge my thinking and who weren't afraid to tell me I had to go back to the proverbial drawing board when I did not get things right. I will always cherish these and future conversations.

A special thanks to Lisa Wolf who was always by my side, never wavering in her good thoughts and willingness to drop everything when I needed help. Mian Shafiq, my personal trainer, kept me sparring in the boxing ring at 6:00 A.M. so I could then go home and focus my writing. Gains!

Heather Jarrow, editor with the Routledge/Taylor & Francis Group, brought clarity of purpose, a strong work ethic, and her goodwill throughout all aspects of getting the book to final form. Heather's feedback on the "almost" final draft of this manuscript was invaluable. The organization and attention to detail provided by Karen Adler, editorial assistant in education, always came at the right time. Really behind the scenes, the production team consisting of Katharine Atherton with the Routledge/Taylor & Francis Group, and John Hodgson, Holly Knapp, Laurence Eastham, and Lois Hall at HWA left no detail unattended. Thank you.

Framing the Issues About Underperforming Teachers

Purpose of the Book—Is the Glass Half-Full or Half-Empty?

The structure and information in this book serve as a bridge between research and practice to help leaders create the "right" conditions for the conversations that are critical in developing a broad range of skills that signal effective teaching. The work of principals and other leaders now must center more fully on the instructional program that is played out in every classroom filled with children who deserve competent, caring, and effective teachers.

Everyone suffers with an underperforming teacher. Students receive sub-par teaching, fellow teachers don't like walking the halls in which an underperforming teacher is assigned, and parents are concerned when their child is assigned to an underperforming teacher's classroom. Administrators have to answer the call to do something about the underperforming teachers in their buildings. More emphatically, school leaders can no longer engage in "passing the trash" or in the "dance of the lemons," allowing underperforming teachers to negatively affect students' ability to reach their full potential (Zepeda, 2013). Mead, Rotherman, and Brown (2012) share that "decades of inattention to teacher performance have been detrimental to students, teachers, and the credibility of the teaching profession" (p. 3). Davis (2013) is resolute that "improving teaching quality and reducing the variability within that quality is a primary responsibility of school district leaders, building level leaders, and teachers" (p. 3). Teachers are the makers or breakers of student success.

This book focuses on school leaders and their work with underperforming teachers because "the fate of our country won't be decided on a battlefield, it will be determined in a classroom" (Weber, 2010, cover page)—a somber thought in light of the responsibility that teachers assume for student learning and the work in which leaders must engage to support all teachers, especially underperforming ones. The helicopter leader who focuses attention on teaching and learning only when there is a problem will not influence teacher development.

This book outlines the critical components framing the processes leaders can follow to work with teachers who have varied instructional, professional, and possibly personal issues that *impede* the overall instructional program. The work is necessary because the impact of underperforming teachers occurs both in and out of the classroom. Although the approaches and strategies offered are geared to work with teachers who are struggling and who, for all practical purposes, can be considered underperforming, most of the ideas can be used universally to support all teachers.

As a leader, take a few minutes to reflect about teachers. In your mind's eye, think about the best teacher you had as a young child. Now take even a few more minutes to think about the worst teacher. These two extreme images of teachers need to be in the forefront of your mind while reading this book and while enacting instructional leadership in your school, where you are more than likely the principal, the assistant principal, or possibly a central office leader who supervises site-level leaders.

Thorny Issue on the Use of Terms

Question: What's in a name? **Answer**: A lot! While framing this book, there were tensions about what word to use to describe teachers with issues— *marginal, incompetent, woeful, sad, borderline, underperforming, sub-par,* or

Table 1.1 Words or Terms Used to Describe Best and Worst Teachers

Words or terms used to describe the best teachers	Words or terms used to describe the worst teachers

struggling? Let's return to the images of the best and the worst teachers. Chances are strong and definitive words and terms emerge to describe the best and the worst teacher you have experienced as a student. Take a minute to jot down (in Table 1.1) a few terms you have used to describe these teacher extremes.

There is a problem when teachers do not make the mark in the classroom. The problem is that the education of children is negatively interrupted and, all too often, gaps in learning are not filled. As a consequence and in many instances, the gaps for some students continue to widen from year to year; the students never catch up. The moral imperatives and the consequences of not working with underperforming teachers are examined more fully in Chapter 9.

Addressing underperformance becomes more important as leaders work in environments that are constantly changing, signaling a need to keep a clear focus on the instructional program and the teachers who have been entrusted to inspire the next generation, our future, to achieve more, to be digital citizens equipped with 21st-century-and-beyond skills, and to be ready with a clear career path when they graduate from high school. Because of the range of possibilities for underperformance, school leaders need a strong command of strategies to detect struggling teachers and to work with them, as well as the resolve to push forward in providing the types of support necessary to make future decisions based on improvement.

The Range of Teaching

In any give school, there are teachers who have varying experiences and exposure to professional learning opportunities, who have journeyed different paths to their entry into teaching (e.g., traditionally certified, alternatively certified), and who are approximations:

- *Teachers who are underperforming* may have learned to "fake it" during classroom observations.

  Sometimes marginal teachers are able to hide because they may have strengths in keeping the peace in the class or they win their students over with low expectations. In the field, these teachers have mastered the dog and pony show, and their performance makes them contenders for a satisfactory or better rating. However, there are some teachers who are highly skilled in one or two areas, yet they have gaps in other areas that are large enough to negatively impact student learning. To do nothing about underperforming teachers puts the school leader in a defenseless position (see Chapter 9). Underperformance left unchecked for any extended time erodes morale, trust, and confidence in building-level, or perhaps system-level, leadership.

- *Teachers who are flat-out incompetent* are unskilled not only in the classroom (hard to prove) but also in the work associated with teaching. This may be demonstrated by not being a team member, not working with colleagues toward school improvement, not following procedures and processes, and not being present because they are chronically absent or show up late, etc.

  So what about the rest of the teachers in the building? They have learning and developmental needs to expand further in their teaching roles and responsibilities. All teachers want to grow, and there are groupings of teachers whose performance ranges from satisfactory-to-good to exceptionally high and accomplished.

- At the mid-range are *teachers who are satisfactory to good*.

  These teachers are average to above-average and, with some coaching and a sincere desire to improve their practices, they can perform at higher levels. But what does average look and sound like in the classroom? Think about the response to this question for a while. Effective teaching and its research base are examined more fully in Chapter 3.

  Willingness has to prevail as the internal motivator to improve. With some gentle nudging in purposeful ways, including support through coaching, online professional development, and the like, these teachers can solidify skills and continually learn from their own practices and from colleagues who can coach them.

- *Teachers who are high performers* are exceptional and accomplished in the classroom.

  These teachers are what I reference as *Kahunas*, a Hawaiian term associated with medical healers that brings with it numerous definitions (Donlin, 2010).

Kahunas have been broadly defined as "magicians" … and "wizards" who are "expert in any profession" (Kahuna, 2004). Teachers who are Kahunas are magical in the classroom, bringing deep understanding of content but, more important, employing instructional strategies that are responsive to the needs of students because they purposefully work to personalize learning and so much more. Teaching and learning in a Kahuna's classroom is transformative for students.

Every parent wants their child to be taught by a Kahuna. Every child deserves to be taught by a highly effective teacher. All school leaders want their teachers to be exemplary in the classroom. Unfortunately, administrators focus their attention on the borderline proficient, the "only acceptable" or, dreadfully speaking, the 15% of the teachers who are woefully underperforming.

Variation in Teaching Skill Ranges

The range of teaching abilities in any given building varies greatly. Research reports that between 5% and 15% of any teaching staff in any school building on the planet ranges from marginal to incompetent (Tucker, 1997, 2001). There is other research that believes the same range is true at the upper levels of accomplished teaching—the Kahunas.

Let's do the math here. If we allow for the upper range of marginal teachers (15%) and the upper range of exemplary teachers (15%), then the rest of the teachers in the building (70%) are proficient, but is being proficient enough? In 2014, the National Center for Education Statistics reported there were 3.1 million full-time teachers in the United States. If 5% to 15% of the 3.1 million full-time teachers are underperforming, the numbers of ineffective teachers could range from between 155,000 to 465,000—what a stark reality given rising accountability.

The Context of Accountability and Teachers

In the world of across-the-system accountability, the work of school leaders is now more central to support the improvement of student, teacher, and school performance. From 1983 with the National Commission on Excellence in Education landmark publication, *A Nation at Risk: The Imperative for Educational*

Reform, to the reauthorization of the Elementary and Secondary Education Act (ESEA), the No Child Left Behind Act of 2001, the emergence of the Race to the Top program, and the flexibility waivers in 2011, accountability has evolved.

No Child Left Behind

The 2001 No Child Left Behind Act (NCLB) put states and school systems on alert that every classroom had to have a highly qualified teacher (Garrett & Steinberg, 2014). Moreover, NCLB instituted provisions for schools to make adequate yearly progress (AYP) and, to make AYP, schools had to close the achievement gap. More on NCLB will be examined in Chapter 2.

Race to the Top and the Elementary and Secondary Education Act Flexibility Waiver

In 2009, the Race to the Top (RTTT) program was initiated as part of the American Recovery and Reinvestment Act (ARRA), funded by the U.S. Department of Education. The focus on teacher and leader evaluation is explicit in the Race to the Top program (Clifford & Ross, 2011). States that received RTTT funding must, according to the *Race to the Top Executive Summary* (U.S. Department of Education, 2009), support leader and teacher evaluation, to

1 Design and implement rigorous, transparent, and fair evaluation systems for teachers and principals that (a) judge effectiveness using multiple rating categories with data on student growth being a significant factor and (b) are designed and developed with involvement by teachers and principals;
2 Conduct annual evaluations that include timely and constructive feedback and, as part of the evaluations, provide teachers and principals with data on student growth for their students, classes, and schools.

(U.S. Department of Education, 2009, p. 9)

No one would argue that teacher and leader evaluation has become complex. Parents, practitioners, and policymakers agree that the key to improving public education in America is placing highly skilled, qualified, and effective teachers in all classrooms (Darling-Hammond, 2010). Chapter 2 examines the basics of teacher evaluation.

Teacher Quality and Teacher Effectiveness

The discussion about teacher effectiveness and teacher quality is important for building-level leaders because, in the final analysis, "they need to be able to identify weaker teachers in order to get them the support they need to join the ranks of effective teachers or to move them out of the classroom if they cannot improve" (Haycock & Hanushek, 2010, p. 49).

Teacher Quality

The U.S. Department of Education (2004) indicates that for teachers to be considered highly qualified, they must (1) have a bachelor's degree, (2) possess full state certification or licensure, and (3) prove that they know each subject they teach. Although a step in the right direction, Toch and Rothman (2008), reported, "Public education defines teacher quality largely in terms of the credentials that teachers have earned, rather than on the basis of the quality of the work they do in their classrooms or the results their students achieve" (p. 2). While mandating that teachers meet those requirements is commendable, there is no mention of teachers being required to demonstrate pedagogical knowledge, content knowledge, or knowledge needed to assess learning (see Chapter 3).

School leaders cannot assume that certification alone makes a teacher highly qualified or that the loopholes through which some teachers enter the profession can ensure that a highly qualified teacher will stand and deliver in a classroom. Darling-Hammond and Baratz-Snowden (2005) report that "at least 50,000 individuals enter teaching each year without training, and most of them are assigned to teach the nation's most vulnerable students in the highest-need schools" (p. 238). The placement of least-qualified teachers in the classroom of students with the highest needs stands in the way of student learning. Goe (2013) is optimistic that if shifts in the purpose and design of teacher evaluation systems occur, teacher evaluation systems could improve teaching through data, feedback that supports growth and development, and professional conversations about student learning.

Teacher Effectiveness

The research base is robust, at times controversial, but always hopeful in looking at what makes a teacher effective. The term *teacher effectiveness* elicits many responses as there are several definitions and ways to examine it. In the context of teacher evaluation systems, Darling-Hammond (2012) indicates that teacher quality "refers to strong instruction that enables a wide range of students to learn" (p. *i*). Hanushek (2010) advocates "the best way to identify a teacher's effectiveness is to observe her classroom performance and specifically what her students learn" (p. 85). One of the biggest takeaways from Hanushek's work is that effectiveness is tied to performance.

Teacher effectiveness is important because a "good run" of teachers "for three or four years" can ameliorate the deficits that children come to school with, and Hanushek (2010) argues that "high-quality teachers can make up for the typical deficits that we see on the preparation of kids from disadvantaged backgrounds (p. 85). Little, Goe, and Bell (2009) note that "teacher effectiveness, in the narrowest sense, refers to a teacher's ability to improve student learning as measured by student gains on standardized achievement tests"; they add, however, that "although this is one important aspect of teaching ability, it is not a comprehensive and robust view of teacher effectiveness" (p. 1). Teacher effectiveness is examined in more detail in Chapter 3.

The New Work of Principals and Assistant Principals

School leaders must now develop their skills as instructional leaders to coach teachers whose skills and talents in and out of the classroom will cover the gamut of underperforming to exceptional and everything in between. School leaders need to know the overall picture of how to work with teachers to get results. School systems can no longer look away because, as Hess and Kelly (2005) remind us, principals "are now pressed both by expectations and by statute to play an increasingly aggressive role in ensuring teacher quality" (p. 38). But it is more than just ensuring teacher quality: It's about teacher effectiveness and whether students are learning. School leaders now must be conversant with the language of teaching and learning; they need to be able to engage in conversations (see Chapter 5) alongside teachers to explore what's working for students.

Leaders need to support teachers in framing the instructional program as it plays out in every classroom. Federal policies, state initiatives, and statutes are in many ways squeezing the life out of teachers, wearing down their resolve to remain in the profession, and distracting them through such constantly moving targets as changing assessments, contentious teacher evaluation systems, and implementation of the Common Core State Standards, which in many ways have distracted schools and leaders from the "core technology of schooling" (Murphy, Elliott, Goldring, & Porter, 2007, p. 179) to meet the needs of every student every day.

Finding the Time

No leader would accept as an excuse from a teacher "I did not teach two out of three required units this year because there was not enough time." Often, principals indicate that they do not have time to supervise instruction, to give feedback on classroom observations, and to engage teachers in professional learning opportunities because they just simply do not have enough time. To be sure, principals are incredibly busy, and they have competing demands on their time; however, it's time to shelve the no-time excuse.

Engaging Stakeholders in Framing the Vision for Teaching and a Common Definition of Good Teaching

McCann, Jones, and Aronoff (2012) tell us that the mission-critical work of the school leader is to engage teachers in the process of

- envisioning what good teaching looks like,
- measuring the quality of current instruction against this standard, and
- working relentlessly to move the quality of instruction closer and closer to the ideal.

At the beginning of this chapter, the reader was asked to think about his or her best and worst teachers. As a leader, what is your vision about exceptional teaching? Do your teachers share that vision of teaching?

As a starting point, take time with the leadership team, such as assistant principals, and map out from your points-of-view what good teaching looks like.

In this vision, what would good teaching look and sound like and what would teachers be doing and saying? What would students be doing in classrooms where good teaching occurs?

Part of a principal's ability to define and describe good teaching is based on being actively involved in classroom observations to see instruction unfold and note the ways in which students are engaged. This means that principals need to stay long enough in classrooms and make a sufficient number of classroom observations daily, weekly, and monthly to inform a definition of good teaching. Moreover, to support effective teaching, principals need to engage in conversations with teachers about effective teaching and other factors that encompass a positive learning environment.

It is one thing for the leader or leadership team to hold a certain vision for teaching and learning, but it is more important to branch out collaboratively to work with teachers on a school-wide vision for teaching and learning. Use time at faculty meetings, grade-level meetings, and any other forum such as team meetings with groups of teachers who collectively work to push forward the instructional program.

It's All About Conversations and Relationships

Chapter 5 focuses on conversations, especially with underperforming teachers. The types of conversations that occur in schools are very much dependent on the culture that has been established, the trust between teachers and leaders, and whether the school embraces risk taking. Conversations about teaching and learning will be open and truthful only if civility, mutual respect, and trust characterize the school's culture. Not all conversations will be happy ones, especially when working with teachers who are struggling in the classroom and who may also be underperforming out of the classroom. However, conversations about teaching and learning are not just for underperforming teachers. All teachers need and want to talk about teaching, what they are doing in their classrooms, and the triumphs and victories as well as the flops when a lesson does not go as planned or when students are getting stuck.

Philip D. Lanoue, the 2015 National American Association of School Administrators (AASA) Superintendent of the Year, serves as the superintendent of the Clarke County School District (Athens, GA). Lanoue was recently quoted in Valerie Strauss's (2015) *Washington Post* blog. Lanoue shared that the main focus of his conversations with his principals is to support them to engage in the talk of teaching with their teachers. Lanoue's conversations with leaders and teachers focus almost exclusively on questions that underscore the connection between teaching and learning, with students at the center of all efforts:

- What do you want kids to know?
- How do you know?
- What do you do when they don't know?
- Do you know them?

(Strauss, 2015, para. 3)

Vigorously Challenging Underperformance in and Out of the Classroom

Courageous conversations, balanced with care and concern for the individual, serve as the compass for the work of school leaders who must become the champions of high-quality teaching. Sugar-coating underperformance in the classroom can no longer be the norm, with the school leader hoping things will get better over time. Underperformance must be couched in a way so that the teacher can understand the situation, corrective action can be taken and, in the end, students are not the victim of a teacher who has serious issues in the classroom.

Teacher evaluation continues to evolve as one mechanism to ensure quality instruction and student growth. The very basics of teacher evaluation are examined in Chapter 2 to give the reader further insight about working with underperforming teachers.

References

American Recovery and Reinvestment Act (ARRA) of 2009, Pub. L. No. 111-5, 123 Stat. 115, 516 (Feb. 19, 2009).

Clifford, M., & Ross, S. (2011). *Designing principal evaluation systems: Research to guide decision-making—Executive summary of current research prepared for the National Association of Elementary School Principals.* Baltimore: Johns Hopkins University. Retrieved from https://www.naesp.org/sites/default/files/PrincipalEvaluation_ ExecutiveSummary.pdf

Darling-Hammond, L. (2010). *Evaluating teacher effectiveness: How teacher performance assessments can measure and improve teaching.* Washington, D.C.: Center for American Progress. Retrieved from www.americanprogress.org

Darling-Hammond, L. (2012). *Creating a comprehensive system for evaluating and supporting effective teaching.* Retrieved from http://edpolicy.stanford.edu/publications/pubs/591

Darling-Hammond, L., & Baratz-Snowden, J. (2005). *A good teacher in every classroom: Preparing the highly-qualified teachers our children deserve.* San Francisco: John Wiley & Sons.

Davis, T. (2013). *McRel's research-based teacher evaluation system: The CUES framework.* Denver: The Center for Educator Effectiveness, McREL International. Retrieved from http://www.mcrel.org/

Donlin, A. (2010). When all the Kahuna are gone: Evaluating Hawaii's traditional Hawaiian healers' law. *Asian-Pacific Law & Policy Journal, 12*(1), 210–248. Retrieved from http://blog.hawaii.edu/aplpj/files/2011/11/APLPJ_12.1_donlin.pdf

Garrett, R., & Steinberg, M. P. (2014). Examining teacher effectiveness using classroom observation scores: Evidence from the randomization of teachers to students. *Educational Evaluation and Policy Analysis, 37*(2), 1–19. doi: 10.3102/0162373714537551

Goe, L. (2013). Can teacher evaluation improve teaching? *Principal Leadership, 13*(7), 24–29. Retrieved from https://www.nassp.org/knowledge-center/publications/principal-leadership

Hanushek, E. A. (2010). The difference is teacher quality. In K. Weber (Ed.), *Waiting for "Superman": How we can save America's failing public schools* (pp. 81–100). New York: Public Affairs.

Haycock, K., & Hanushek, E. A. (2010). An effective teacher in every classroom. *Education Next, 10*(3), 46–52. Retrieved from http://hanushek.stanford.edu/publications/teacher-quality

Hess, F. M., & Kelly, A. P. (2005). The accidental principal: What doesn't get taught at ed schools? *Education Next, 5*(3), 34–40. Retrieved from http://educationnext.org/

Kahuna. 2004. In *Ulukau: Hawaiian dictionary.* Retrieved from http://wehewehe.org/gsdl2.85/cgi-bin/hdict?e=q-11000-00---off-0hdict--00-1----0-10-0---0---0direct-10-ED--4-------0-1lpm--11-haw-Zz-1---Zz-1-home-k%C4%81huna--00-3-1-00-0--4----0-0-11-00-0utfZz-8-00&a=d&d=D6052

Little, O., Goe, L., & Bell, C. (2009). *A practical guide to evaluating teacher effectiveness.* Washington, D.C.: National Comprehensive Center for Teacher Quality. Retrieved from http://www.gtlcenter.org/sites/default/files/docs/practicalGuide.pdf

McCann, T. M., Jones, A. C., & Aronoff, G. A. (2012). *Teaching matters most: A school leader's guide to improving classroom instruction.* Thousand Oaks, CA. Corwin.

Mead, S., Rotherman, A., & Brown, R. (2012). *The hangover: Thinking about the unintended consequences of the Nation's teacher evaluation binge.* Washington, D.C.: American Enterprise Institute. Retrieved from https://www.aei.org

Murphy, J., Elliott, S. N., Goldring, E., & Porter, A. C. (2007). Leadership for learning: A research-based model and taxonomy of behaviors. *School Leadership and Management, 27*(2), 179–201. doi: 10.1080/13632430701237420

National Center for Education Statistics. (2014). *Fast facts.* Washington, D.C.: Institute for Education Sciences. Retrieved from http://nces.ed.gov/fastfacts/display.asp?id=28

National Commission on Excellence in Education. (1983). *A nation at risk: The imperative for educational reform: A report to the Nation and the Secretary of Education, United States Department of Education.* Washington, D.C.: The Commission. Retrieved from http://eric.ed.gov/?id=ED226006

No Child Left Behind (NCLB) Act of 2001, Pub. L. No. 107–110, § 115, Stat. 1425.

Strauss, V. (2015, June 10). 2015 National superintendent of the year teaches for a day. Here's what he learned. *The Washington Post*. Retrieved from http://www.washingtonpost.com/blogs/answer-sheet/wp/2015/06/10/2015-national-superintendent-of-the-year-teaches-for-a-day-heres-what-he-learned/

Toch, T., & Rothman, R. (2008). *Rush to judgment: Teacher evaluation in public education*. Washington, D.C.: Education Sector at the American Institutes for Research. Retrieved from https://www.sde.idaho.gov/site/charter_schools/research/Administrator/Rush%20to%20Judgement%20Teacher%20Evaluation.pdf

Tucker, P. D. (1997). Lake Wobegon: Where all teachers are competent (or, have we come to terms with the problem of incompetent teachers?). *Journal of Personnel Evaluation in Education 11*(2), 103–126. doi: 10.1023/A:1007962302463

Tucker, P. (2001). Helping struggling teachers. *Educational Leadership, 58*(5), 52–55. Retrieved from http://www.ascd.org/publications/educational-leadership.aspx

U.S. Department of Education. (2004). *New No Child Left Behind flexibility: Highly qualified teachers*. Washington, D.C.: U.S. Department of Education. Retrieved from http://www2.ed.gov/nclb/methods/teachers/hqtflexibility.html

U.S. Department of Education. (2009). *Race to the Top program executive summary*. Retrieved from http://www2.ed.gov/programs/racetothetop/executive-summary.pdf

U.S. Department of Education. (2011). *Laws and guidance/elementary and secondary education, ESEA flexibility*. Retrieved from http://www2.ed.gov/policy/elsec/guid/esea-flexibility/flex-renewal/index.html?exp=0

Weber, K. (Ed.). (2010). *Waiting for "Superman": How we can save America's failing public schools*. New York: Public Affairs.

Zepeda, S. J. (2013). *The principal as instructional leader: A practical handbook* (3rd ed.). New York: Routledge.

2 Teacher Evaluation in a Nutshell

At the writing of this book, President Obama had just signed into law the Every Student Succeeds Act (2015; known as ESSA), the reauthorization of the Elementary and Secondary Education Act (1965), replacing the defunct No Child Left Behind Act (2001) and the waivers associated with the American Reinvestment Stimulus found in the Race to the Top program. The provisions of the Every Student Succeeds Act go into effect in 2016–2017. The waivers associated with the Race to the Top program incentivized states to develop rigorous teacher and leader evaluation systems that coupled student results on standardized tests to individual teachers.

The Every Student Succeeds Act does not mandate teacher or leader evaluations; instead, ESSA leaves the policies related to the evaluation of teachers and leaders to the discretion of the states, and removes the requirement that they use standardized test results to evaluate teachers. The shifts in power now situate states as the major decision makers in matters related to teacher and leader evaluation.

With confidence, I believe that teacher evaluation systems will shift, but in what direction, time will only tell. To this end, school leaders need to keep abreast of changes at the state level and how these amendments of policy might impact teacher and leader evaluation systems and the practices at the local level. With confidence, the materials in this chapter and offered throughout this book will stand the test of time and will bring clarity to the work needed to support underperformance.

The face of teacher evaluation was influenced first by the No Child Left Behind Act of 2001 (NCLB) with its call for highly qualified teachers in a standards-based classroom. The Race to the Top program (RTTT), with its focus on teacher effectiveness, situated teacher evaluation at its center. The voluntary Elementary and Secondary Education Act (ESEA) waiver from NCLB and the stipulations found with adequate yearly progress for states who adopted rigorous teacher evaluation systems included matching student success on standardized tests with a teacher's effectiveness.

With the flurry of federal and state activity, there are some new "basics" related to teacher evaluation and the importance of looking at multiple data points throughout the process. The ability to enact teacher evaluation resides in large part in the knowledge and understanding of effective teaching. There are many ways in which underperforming teachers can be detected. One way to unearth underperformance is through a leader's informal and formal classroom observations in which he or she can see and hear instruction unfold, with one eye focused on the teacher and the other eye focused on what students are learning in the classroom environment. However, teacher evaluation systems now include much more than classroom observations.

No Child Left Behind Act of 2001 and Race to the Top

NCLB set the stage for focusing on teacher quality, implementing research-based instructional strategies, increasing a standards-based focus especially in mathematics and science, and developing statewide assessments of student learning. The U.S. Congress appropriated more than $5 billion between 2009 and 2012 to the RTTT program to support states and school systems in focusing their attention on designing, developing, and implementing programs and processes to evaluate teachers and principals. The thought is that teacher effectiveness can be enhanced through evaluation systems. In 2011, voluntary flexibility waiver opportunities were offered to all states (not just to RTTT states) by the U.S. Department of Education (2014).

No Child Left Behind

NCLB was the reauthorization of the 1965 ESEA. Through NCLB, states were required to hold students accountable by testing them in reading and math in grades 3 through 8 and again, once, in high school. The testing regimen was intended to focus attention on closing student achievement gaps and to provide all students with an education that was fair and equal. States had to develop academic standards and a state testing system to meet the federal requirements. As discussed in Chapter 1, the provisions of NCLB focused on ensuring that schools had highly qualified teachers; however, these provisions do not necessarily lead to effective teaching or address teacher effectiveness.

Race to the Top

Teacher and leader evaluation is at the forefront of just about every school, system, and state since the inception and implementation of the waiver, RTTT, that released states and their schools from the sanctions of NCLB. The RTTT program was created by the Obama administration under the American Recovery and Reinvestment Act (ARRA) of 2009. In 2009, when the RTTT was announced, one of the primary goals included revising teacher evaluation systems and processes that would include, for example, more uses of student performance data in the overall assessment for individual teachers. Essentially, student achievement data would be linked to individual teachers, and the growth (or lack of it) would be attributed to teacher performance. The RTTT grant application held criteria for the evaluation of teachers. RTTT applications had to address plans to

1 Establish clear approaches to measuring student achievement growth for individual students.
2 Design and implement rigorous, transparent, and fair evaluation systems for teachers.
3 Differentiate effectiveness using multiple rating categories that take student achievement growth into account as a significant factor and are designed with teacher involvement.
4 Conduct annual evaluations that include timely and constructive feedback and provide teachers with data on student achievement growth for their students, classes, and schools.

5 Use evaluations to inform decisions about staff development, compensation, promotion, tenure, certification, and removal of ineffective teachers.

(Hallgren, James-Burduny, & Perez-Johnson, 2014, p. 2)

Race to the Top and the Changing Landscape of Teacher Evaluation

The uses of value-added methods and models are controversial, and there has been a backlash from learned societies (American Statistical Association, 2014) and researchers (Darling-Hammond, 2012; Darling-Hammond, Amrein-Beardsley, Haertel, & Rothstein, 2011; Koretz, 2008). Regardless of whether the uses of student data linked to teacher practice are championed or opposed, the reality is that teacher (and leader) evaluation has changed significantly and rapidly since 2009. The results of Weisberg, Sexton, Mulhern, and Keeling's study (2009) were based on data from across 4 states in 12 districts that included 15,000 teachers and 1,300 principals. The results of this study give a face to the woeful condition of teacher and leader evaluations in which all personnel are treated like "widgets"—all the same, in effect. To highlight, Weisberg et al. (2009) found that

- **All teachers are rated good or great**. Less than 1 percent of teachers receive unsatisfactory ratings, making it impossible to identify truly exceptional teachers.
- **Excellence goes unrecognized**. Fifty-nine percent of teachers and 63 percent of administrators say their district is not doing enough to identify, compensate, promote, and retain the most effective teachers.
- **Professional development is inadequate.** Almost 3 in 4 teachers did not receive any specific feedback on improving their performance in their last evaluation.
- **Novice teachers are neglected.** Low expectations for beginning teachers translate into benign neglect in the classroom and a toothless tenure process.
- **Poor performance goes unaddressed.** Half of the districts studied have not dismissed a single tenured teacher for poor performance in the past five years.

(p. 6, emphasis added)

These results are troubling across the board; however, the pervasiveness of the findings related to performance going unaddressed are amplified even more by Weisberg et al. (2009) who report that

> Despite uniformly positive evaluation ratings, teachers and administrators both recognize ineffective teaching in their schools. In fact, 81 percent of administrators and 57 percent of teachers say there is a tenured teacher in their school who is performing poorly, and 43 percent of teachers say there is a tenured teacher who should be dismissed for poor performance. Troublingly, the percentages are higher in high-poverty schools. But district records confirm the scarcity of formal dismissals; at least half of the districts studied did not dismiss a single non-probationary teacher for poor performance in the time period studied (ranging from two to five years in each district).
>
> (p. 6)

These findings help to frame the need for more responsive supervisory practices that are developmental and differentiated and for professional learning that is job embedded and responsive to adult learners as a means to support growth and development. Related to underperforming teachers, comprehensive teacher evaluation systems can do one of two things—support teachers in improving or lead the way to progressively intensifying assistance that could end in a recommendation not to renew a teacher's contract.

Teacher Evaluation—The Basics

Teacher evaluation systems have become complex, especially in tying student achievement outcomes on high-stakes tests to teacher ratings, including multiple sources of data (e.g., student surveys, artifacts, and evidence) along with the mainstay practices such as multiple classroom observations. The conversation about teacher evaluation has changed dramatically with

- the emergence of value-added methods and measures where standardized test percentages are being applied to teacher's summative evaluation;
- the results of surveys students complete about their teachers' performance being factored into a teacher's summative evaluation;
- the use of artifacts and evidence being routinely examined; and

- regularly scheduled classroom observations and other parts of the evaluation system being enacted in such a way that school leaders can provide timely feedback to teachers.

Teacher evaluation has become a hands-on process and a priority area for leaders to fulfill the requirements that, in many states, are logged into a statewide electronic platform, with metrics detailing progress in the systems mandated by local state departments of education. Both teachers and leaders use these platforms to review formative data that trails to the summative evaluation.

Examination of the basics of teacher evaluation can help the school leader be ready to work in appropriate ways with teachers and the instructional program. Teacher evaluation is not just a weeding-out process; however, without presence and firsthand knowledge of teachers and their practices and the results they achieve, leaders will not be able to detect underperforming teaching and will be unable to recognize and celebrate exemplary teaching. The reader is encouraged to examine state-level policies, regulations, and legislation because these documents ultimately frame and specify practices related to teacher and leader evaluation with which systems must comply.

Formative and Summative Tug-of-War

In the world of instructional supervision, there has been a tug-of-war relationship between the formative and summative aspects associated with supervision and evaluation (Zepeda, 2012, 2013; Zepeda, Lanoue, Price, & Jimenez, 2014). The belief is that the evaluator (principal, assistant principal) cannot render formative assessments and then shift gears to deliver a summative verdict about a teacher's performance without experiencing role conflict, eroding trust, and sending mixed messages. The reality is that school leadership teams are just not big enough to have one person engage in formative support and another school leader repeat the work necessary to render a summative assessment.

Popham (2013) traces the tensions between formative and summative evaluation, asking school leaders to engage in both but to do so "separately," offering this sage counsel:

> The unthinking mixture of formative and summative teacher evaluation will almost certainly foster inappropriate teacher evaluations. But because formative and summative teacher evaluation can each make significant

contributions to instruction, both should be implemented widely—but separately—as components of emerging teacher-evaluation systems.

(p. 22)

In other words, leaders must enact with fidelity formative aspects of evaluation, holding these insights as a way to arrive at a summative point in the evaluation. Formative and summative evaluation have different intents. An apt metaphor to delineate the differences between formative and summative evaluation was offered by Robert Stake (as cited in Scriven, 1991, p. 19) who shared, "When the cook tastes the soup, that's formative; when the guests taste the soup, that's summative."

Formative Evaluation

The word *formative* is synonymous with *developmental*, *constructive*, and *improvement*. Formative evaluation is continuous and offers feedback along the way. Formative evaluation gives the leader and teacher time to gather information, to discuss progress toward goals, and to get a clear picture of the types of professional learning opportunities that would be helpful based on performance. During formative evaluation, the principal and teacher have the opportunity to identify and better understand strengths and weaknesses and, moreover, to plan ways of supporting growth in areas that need development (Popham, 2013; Scriven, 1991).

The processes that could be part of a formative evaluation system include classroom observations, examination of student artifacts, and discussions around instructional practices with colleagues. Teachers could also engage in observing colleagues who have strength in a targeted area, engage in peer coaching, participate in a book study, shadow team members, or start an action research project. This list could be expanded by examining the programs available at the site, across the district, and throughout the region, including tapping into online and digital resources.

Summative Evaluation

A summative evaluation signals an end to the formative process. The primary intents of evaluation are to meet state statutes and district policies, assign teachers a rating at the end of the year and, in some cases, determine whether a teacher will return to work the following year.

A summative evaluation should include data from numerous sources—classroom observations (formal and informal), artifacts and evidence (lesson plan exemplars, student work samples), student surveys, and data from standardized tests (how well did students perform); in a case where there is no standardized test (e.g., band, electronics, art, etc.), results on student learning objectives (SLOs) are associated with a teacher's summative evaluation judgment for the year. The use of student achievement data vis-à-vis value-added measures (VAMs) factored into a teacher's summative evaluation has caused both praise and furor among teachers, leaders, policymakers, and researchers.

Value-Added Measures

The accountability reforms—namely, RTTT and waivers—presently dictate that for statewide teacher evaluation systems, student achievement as measured by tests be factored in the overall evaluation for teachers and leaders. For example, in the state of Georgia, 50% of a teacher's summative evaluation is based on a single test and 70% of a leader's evaluation is based on what students do in the buildings in which they lead. VAMs are not new, and these measures have been used widely in a few states for about the last 10 years.

The Glossary of Education Reform (2013) provides an overview of VAMs:

- Value-added measures, or *growth measures*, are used to estimate or quantify how much of a positive (or negative) effect individual teachers have on student learning during the course of a given school year. To produce the estimates, value-added measures typically use sophisticated statistical algorithms and standardized-test results, combined with other information about students, to determine a "value-added score" for a teacher.

    (para. 1, emphasis in the original)

- Value-added measures employ mathematical algorithms in an attempt to isolate an individual teacher's contribution to student learning from all the other factors that can influence academic achievement and progress—e.g., individual student ability, family income levels, the educational attainment of parents, or the influence of peer groups.

    (para. 2)

- By only comparing a teacher's effect on student learning against other teachers working with similar types of students, value-added systems attempt to avoid comparisons that would be perceived as unfair (although the fairness and reliability of such calculations is a matter of ongoing dispute). The measurements typically attempt to quantify how much more (or less) student achievement improved in comparison to what would be expected based on past test scores and personal and demographic factors. While value-added measures use many different algorithms and statistical methods to gauge teacher effectiveness, most of them consider the past test scores of a teacher's students.

(para. 3)

The Potential Uses of Value-Added Measures

VAMs can control for multiple factors that impact student test scores and therefore offer an estimate of how a teacher is teaching in a particular year. Value-added models can be reliable because they allow systems to look beyond single measures to evaluate a teacher's effectiveness. Moreover, value-added models are particularly effective when they are used to supplement information gathered during a performance evaluation system (Weisberg et al., 2009). However, these opinions are not universally held.

The Potential Abuses of Value-Added Measures

Darling-Hammond (2012), from a synthesis of research, posits that there are at least three fundamental flaws with the practice of using VAMs and models for assessing teachers as part of a teacher evaluation system. These fundamental flaws include

1 *Value-Added Models (VAM) of Teacher Effectiveness Are Highly Unstable.* Teachers' ratings differ substantially from *class to class* and from *year to year,* as well as from one *test* to the next.
2 *Teachers' Value-Added Ratings Are Significantly Affected by Differences in the Students Who Are Assigned to Them.* Even when models try to control for prior achievement and student demographic variables, teachers are advantaged or disadvantaged based on the students they teach. In particular, teachers with large numbers of new English learners

and others with special needs have been found to show lower gains than the same teachers when they are teaching other students.

3 *Value-Added Ratings Cannot Disentangle the Many Influences on Student Progress.* Many other home, school, and student factors influence student learning gains, and these matter more than the individual teacher in explaining changes in scores.

(p. ii, emphasis in the original)

Seeing Beyond Value-Added Measures

Embedded in valid teacher evaluation systems is a research base on effective teaching and learning systems. Student learning is the center of all efforts for systems and their teachers and would include, for example, "common statewide standards for teaching" (Darling-Hammond, 2012) as the foundation for anchoring evidence related to student learning. Beyond the single assessment, evidence of student learning should include teacher judgment (Darling-Hammond, Amrein-Beardsley, Haertel, & Rothstein, 2012; Darling-Hammond, 2012) as well as other sources of evidence, possibly including

- External test measures, such as Measure of Academic Progress (MAP) scores from fall and winter
- Classroom tests or other periodic assessments that show growth in academic understanding/skills on specific concepts
- Student papers/products that show growth or mastery of academic understanding/skills
- Student work samples that illustrate student learning through revision of work or repeated practice on similar concept
- Student reflections on their learning (e.g., through logs, journals, portfolios)
- Student exhibitions or major assessments.

(Oregon Department of Education, n.d.)

From these examples of evidence, there are several patterns to note. The evidence is varied and follows the acts of teaching and learning. If evidence is predicated on goals and standards, then evidence would also follow a trail of differentiation—tasks and evidence that grow more complex as students are learning. Evidence would be collected throughout the year, not just at the beginning and then at the end of the year.

Getting Teacher Evaluation Right

Teacher evaluation done right supports teachers in the development and refinement of practices using both formative and summative assessments. However, teacher evaluation often lacks credibility in that "[o]nly 43 percent of teachers agree that evaluation helps teachers improve" (Weisberg et al., 2009, p. 14) and, all too often, "Excellence goes unrecognized, development is neglected and poor performance goes unaddressed" (p. 10). Callahan and Sadeghi (2014) summarize that teacher evaluation systems have failed because "teachers do not receive the feedback they need, and professional development is not aligned with areas of need" (p. 729).

For teachers, the processes of teacher evaluation systems can increase self-awareness of strengths and areas that need support. Teacher evaluation systems enable leaders to enact their role of ensuring that the instructional program is being carried out by a competent teacher and that underperforming teachers are able to get the support they need to improve or are counseled out of the position or, possibly, even the profession.

The results of formative and summative evaluation can be used to determine professional development needs not only for individual teachers but also for groups of teachers across grade levels or subject areas. Increased awareness of strengths and weaknesses can support the necessary actions needed for school improvement as well.

Supervision That Supports Teachers

Teachers need differentiated and developmental approaches to supervision and support. It is often a struggle for schools and districts to adjust to the diversity of teaching practices that exist within one system, particularly amid rapidly changing performance measures that make it daunting to keep one's finger on the pulse of the types of professional development and other supports needed to forward teacher effectiveness.

As a supervisor, teachers need timely and specific feedback (see Chapter 5) that is aligned with teacher evaluation and that promotes reflection (Schooling, Toth, & Marzano, 2010; Zepeda, 2012). Teachers want supervisors who are present (Zepeda & Ponticell, 1998), who have built relationships based on trust (Tschannen-Moran, 2014), and who have at heart the teachers' best interest, wanting to see them improve with the appropriate supports. Teachers need opportunities to:

Figure 2.1 Formative Supervisory Supports for Underperforming Teachers

- observe other teachers and to engage in reflective conversations about the work of teaching;
- wrestle with difficult problems in a fault-free environment so they can take calculated risks;
- engage in conversations and receive honest feedback about performance (Zepeda et al., 2014); and
- feel there is hope that they can improve.

The most at-risk and underperforming teachers need supportive and formative supervision to succeed. Figure 2.1 identifies some of the types of supervisory supports that can be effective for all teachers but, most especially, for underperforming teachers.

What's Your Supervisory Approach?

No two leaders will share the same approaches or have the same style of working with teachers. The supervisory approach taken with teachers is dependent on the conditions within the building, the relationships that leaders have established with teachers, and the teachers' needs. The needs of teachers vary and no two teachers are alike—that is, everyone has different needs that must be met. Effective leaders know their teachers individually and collectively. Without such knowledge, interventions of support for underperforming teachers will likely be too generic.

Responses to Working with Underperforming Teachers

Underperforming teachers present challenges and opportunities for the school leadership. In later chapters, many of the challenges and opportunities are discussed in detail. For now, let's look at four possible responses to dealing with underperforming teachers:

1   Ignore the problems in hopes that they will go away: The problems of underperforming teachers will not magically disappear; in fact, left unchecked, the problems associated with underperformance will only intensify, leading to more problems.
2   Confront the issue square on and provide intensive assistance: Given the ethical and moral issues and the deleterious impact ineffective teachers have on students and, in many cases, on the overall school, this is really the only way to ensure students have a chance to succeed now and in the future.
3   Delegate the problem to someone else: Although the principal may choose to enlist the support of others in working with underperforming teachers, delegation is not the problem. Delegating the work needed to support underperforming teachers signals "washing your hands of the issue." This is bad for teacher morale.
4   Pass off the underperforming teacher to a different school within or outside of the system: Passing the trash only hands the problems and challenges to someone else.

Professional Development That Embraces Adult Learning

The intents and purposes of teacher evaluation are to promote growth and development, to celebrate best practices, and to ensure that teachers are doing their absolute best teaching that leads to student learning and growth. However, another purpose is to offer remediation to teachers who are struggling and, if necessary, to move to a non-renewal recommendation.

Professional learning supports and anchors formative and summative evaluation, because once strengths or areas in need of improvement are identified, both the teacher and leader can begin framing a plan of action to address these areas. Professional learning will become especially important as plans of improvement (remediation plans) are developed with underperforming teachers (see Chapter 6).

For the underperforming teacher, the school leader has access to data from several sources including, but not limited to, classroom observations, results of student achievement measures, samples of student work, and student survey results. External to the classroom, data could include the number, frequency, and types of discipline referrals, written concerns from parents and students, observation of the teacher during team and grade-level data meetings, and a self-generated portfolio, to name a few.

It is through the data that targets for professional learning can be identified that are content-based and based on the needs of the teacher. In Table 2.1, the commonalities between the principles of adult learning and job-embedded learning are presented, with applications that could be used with underperforming teachers.

Research and Best Practices Related to High-Quality Professional Learning

If we want our teachers to be highly effective and to move the needle toward increasing student achievement, we owe it to teachers to provide the very best practices associated with professional learning. Here is what the research and literature tells us about professional learning that supports teacher development:

- Professional learning extends over time and allows teachers sufficient time to interact with resources (Darling-Hammond & McLaughlin, 2011).
- Professional learning must be continuous, ongoing, and with follow-up a part of the process (Darling-Hammond & Falk, 2013).
- Professional learning is embedded within the workday and relevant to what is going on in teachers' classrooms (Zepeda, 2015).
- Professional learning is content- and grade-specific to teachers' subject matter (Desimone, 2011).
- Professional learning promotes collaboration, brainstorming, reflection, and inquiry (Timperley, 2008).
- Professional learning employs varied learning strategies for adults (Drago-Severson, 2009).
- Professional learning is grounded in student data (Darling-Hammond & McLaughlin, 2011).

Table 2.1 Commonalities Between Adult Learning and Job-Embedded Learning

Principles of adult learning	Principles of job-embedded learning
Make learning both an active and an interactive process.	Holds relevance for the adult learner: Adults want to be successful and derive value from their learning. Job-embedded learning is highly individualized.
Provide hands-on, concrete experiences, and real-life experiences.	Job-embedded learning includes feedback and collaborative supports as built-in process (e.g., peer coaching or reflection journals).
Employ novelty, but also connect to the adult learners' prior experiences and knowledge.	Supports inquiry and reflection: Job-embedded learning promotes thinking more critically and reflectively about practice. This can be done at the individual level or as a group.
Give them opportunities to apply the new knowledge to what they already know or have experienced.	Facilitates the transfer of new skills into practice: Job-embedded learning provides ongoing support, which is linked to transferring learned skills into practice.
Use a variety of approaches to accommodate different learning styles and experiences and use examples.	Promotes collaboration: It is through collaboration that teachers share with one another, engage in discussions, and reflect about their experiences.
Use small-group activities through which learners have the opportunity to reflect, analyze, and practice what they have learned.	
Provide coaching, technical assistance, feedback, or other follow-up support as part of the training.	
Give adult learners as much control as possible over what they learn, how they learn, and other aspects of the learning experience.	
Source: Roberts and Pruitt (2009, p. 75)	*Source:* Zepeda (2015, pp. 35–38)

Applications for underperforming teachers
• Professional development (PD) is differentiated and based on experience levels.   • PD is steeped in a content area with accompanying instructional strategies.   • Modeling of skills and concepts occurs.   • Coaching is provided to support transfer of skills and knowledge to the content of a teacher's situation.   • Goals and targets are set.   • Continuous feedback is provided.   • Reflection and refinement are encouraged.   • Resources are available.   • Colleagues engage in the work with underperforming teachers in non-evaluative ways.

- Professional learning is evaluated and assessed (Zepeda, 2012).
- Professional learning is coherent, linking to other processes such as teacher evaluation, supervision, and other support programs for teachers (Zepeda, 2012, 2015).

Professional development that supports learning is job embedded, allowing teachers to gain insights from the work they do in classrooms and with colleagues.

Job-Embedded Learning

Teachers learn to teach as they move through their careers, and one of the most powerful forms of professional development is when learning activities are embedded within the workday. Job-embedded professional development "refers to teacher learning that is grounded in day-to-day teaching practice and is designed to enhance teachers' content-specific instructional practices with the intent of improving student learning" (Croft, Coggshall, Dolan, Power, & Killion, 2010, p. 2). Teachers learn from interacting with their peers "around teaching and learning, including conversations about instruction, peer observations, feedback, and advice-seeking about instruction" (Parise & Spillane, 2010, p. 324).

In a response to the report *The Mirage: Confronting the Hard Truth about the Quest for Teacher Development*, Learning Forward (formerly the National Staff Development Council) released a statement (2015) indicating that

1 Professional learning must result in demonstrable evidence of improved teaching and learning.
2 Personalized professional learning, aligned with school and system goals, leads to improvements in teaching and learning.
3 The system for professional learning must be reimagined. While we have thought for years that we know what it takes to help people improve, the evidence doesn't support it. We must get serious about creating the systems of support that our teachers and students need most.

(para. 6–8)

The next logical area to examine is teaching and learning as evaluation systems focus attention on what effective teachers do in the classroom. Chapter 3 focuses on effective teaching.

References

American Recovery and Reinvestment Act (ARRA) of 2009, Pub. L. No. 111-5, 123 Stat. 115, 516 (Feb. 19, 2009).

American Statistical Association. (2014). *ASA statement on using value-added models for educational assessment.* Alexandria, VA. Author. Retrieved from httw/www.amstat.org

Callahan, K., & Sadeghi, L. (2014). TEACHNJ: An evaluation of two years of implementation. *US-China Education Review A, 4*(10), 728–736. Retrieved from http://www.davidpublisher.org

Croft, A., Coggshall, J. G., Dolan, M., Powers, E., & Killion, J. (2010). *Job-embedded professional development: What it is, who is responsible, and how to get it done well* [Issue brief]. Washington, D.C.: National Comprehensive Center for Teacher Quality.

Darling-Hammond, L. (2012). *Creating a comprehensive system for evaluating an supporting effective teaching.* Stanford: Stanford Center for Opportunity Policy in Education. Retrieved from https://edpolicy.stanford.edu/sites/default/files/publications/creating-comprehensive-system-evaluating-and-supporting-effective-teaching.pdf

Darling-Hammond, L., Amrein-Beardsley, A., Haertel, E. H., & Rothstein, J. (2011). *Getting teacher evaluation right: A background paper for policy makers.* Washington, D.C.: American Educational Research Association and the National Academy of Education.

Darling-Hammond, L., Amrein-Beardsley, A., Haertel, E. H., & Rothstein, J. (2012). Evaluating teacher evaluation. *Phi Delta Kappan, 93*(6), 8–15. doi:10.1177/003172171209300603

Darling-Hammond, L., & Falk, B. (2013). *Teacher learning: How student-performance assessments can support teacher learning.* Washington, D.C.: Center for American Progress.

Darling-Hammond, L., & McLaughlin, M. W. (2011). Policies that support professional development in an era of reform. *Phi Delta Kappan, 92*(6), 81–92. Retrieved from www.pdkintl.org/publications/kappan

Desimone, L. M. (2011). A primer on effective professional development. *Phi Delta Kappan, 92*(6), 68–71. doi: 10.2307/25822820

Drago-Severson, E. (2009). *Leading adult learning: Supporting adult development in our schools.* Thousand Oaks, CA: Corwin.

Elementary and Secondary Education Act (ESEA) of 1965, Pu. L. 89-10, 79 Stat. 27 (April 11, 1965).

Every Student Succeeds Act (ESSA) of 2015, Pub. L. No. 114-95 Stat. 1177.

Glossary of Education Reform. (2013). *Value-added measures.* Retrieved on July 11, 2015 from http://edglossary.org/value-added-measures

Hallgren, K., James-Burduny, S., & Perez-Johnson, I. (2014). *State requirements for teacher evaluation policies promoted by Race to the Top.* Washington, D.C.: National Center for Education Evaluation Institute for Education Sciences. Retrieved from http://files.eric.ed.gov/fulltext/ED544794.pdf

Koretz, D. (2008). A measured approach: Value-added models are a promising improvement, but no one measure can evaluate teacher performance. *American Educator, 32*(3), 18–27. Retrieved from http://www.aft.org/our-news/periodicals/american-educator

Learning Forward. (2015, August 4). *From mirage to reality: Redesign professional learning to improve classroom teaching.* Oxford, OH: Author. Available at www.learningforward.org/who-we-are/announcements/press-releases/2015/08/04/from-mirage-to-reality-redesign-professional-learning-to-improve-classroom-teaching

No Child Left Behind (NCLB) Act of 2001, Pub. L. No. 107-110, § 115, Stat. 1425.

Oregon Department of Education. (n.d.). *Looking at student learning.* Retrieved from http://www.ode.state.or.us/wma/teachlearn/educatoreffectiveness/studentlearningevidence.pdf

Parise, L. M., & Spillane, J. P. (2010). Teacher learning and instructional change: How formal and on-the-job learning opportunities predict changes in elementary school teachers' instructional practice. *Elementary School Journal, 110*(3), 323–346. doi: 10.1086/648981

Popham, W. J. (2013). On serving two masters: Formative and summative evaluation. *Principal Leadership, 13*(7), 18–22. Retrieved from http://www.nassp.org/tabid/3788/default.aspx?topic=On_Serving_Two_Masters

Roberts, S. M., & Pruitt, E. Z. (2009). *Schools as professional learning communities: Collaborative activities and strategies for professional development.* Thousand Oaks, CA: Corwin.

Schooling, P., Toth, M., & Marzano, R. J. (2010). *Creating an aligned system to develop teachers within the federal Race to the Top initiative* [White paper]. Englewood, CO: Marzano Research Laboratory. Retrieved from http://www.marzanoresearch.com/free_resources/selected_research.aspx

Scriven, M. (1991). Beyond formative and summative evaluation. In J. S. Wholey, H. P. Hatry, & K. E. Newcomer (Eds.), *Evaluation and education: A quarter century* (pp. 19–64). Chicago: University of Chicago Press.

Timperley, H. (2008). *National education findings of assess to learn (AtoL) report.* Wellington, New Zealand: Ministry of Education.

Tschannen-Moran, M. (2014). *Trust matters: Leadership for successful schools* (2nd ed.). San Francisco: Jossey-Bass.

U.S. Department of Education. (2014). *ESEA flexibility: Guidance for renewal process.* Washington, D.C.: Office of the Secretary and Office of Public Affairs. Retrieved from http://www2.ed.gov/policy/elsec/guid/esea-flexibility/index.html

Weisberg, D., Sexton, S., Mulhern, J., & Keeling, D. (2009). *The widget effect: Our national failure to acknowledge and act on differences in teacher effectiveness.* Brooklyn, NY: The New Teacher Project. Retrieved from http://carnegie.org/fileadmin/Media/Publications/widget.pdf

Zepeda, S. J. (2012). *Instructional supervision: Applying tools and concepts* (3rd ed.). New York: Routledge.

Zepeda, S. J. (2013). *The principal as instructional leader: A practical handbook* (3rd ed.). New York: Routledge.

Zepeda, S. J. (2015). *Job-embedded professional development: Support, collaboration, and learning in schools.* New York: Routledge.

Zepeda, S. J., & Ponticell, J.A. (1998). At cross-purposes: What do teachers need, want, and get from supervision? *Journal of Curriculum and Supervision, 14*(1), 68–87. Retrieved from http://www.ascd.org/publications/jcs/archived-issues.aspx

Zepeda, S. J., Lanoue, P. D., Price, N. F., & Jimenez, A. M. (2014). Principal evaluation—Linking individual and building-level progress: Making the connections and embracing the tensions. *School Leadership and Management Journal, 34*(4), 324–351. doi:10.1080/13632434.2014.928681

Making the Commitment to Effective Teaching

3

This chapter examines effective teaching because learning to teach

- is a life-long endeavor that can be supported by effective teacher evaluation practice;
- means extending and modifying instruction based on the results achieved in the classroom; and
- is a reciprocal process in which teachers learn from their students as students learn, grapple, and gain mastery of content that is bundled within the curriculum.

Teacher evaluation, by its very intents, is about improving teaching. Leaders engage in many activities to assess teacher effectiveness. A mainstay process of any teacher evaluation system is the classroom observation in which the leader spends time watching instruction unfold and students interact with the teacher, the content, and instruction. Teacher effectiveness can be examined through other processes in which data can be collected, analyzed, and discussed with teachers (results of student surveys, results of statewide tests administered to students, goals set forth by teachers, etc.). Almost all of these processes can lead to examining teacher effectiveness.

Effective Teachers

Teaching matters because we lose students through outdated teaching approaches (Noguera & Wing, 2006). Students have spoken out about the quality of teaching, reporting that most instruction is not relevant and is de-motivating and, according to Bridgeland, Dilulio, and Morrison (2006), who reported the perspectives of 470 high school dropouts, 50% thought classes were boring and not relevant to their lives and/or career aspirations and 67% indicated they would have worked harder to graduate if teachers had been more demanding and provided the necessary supports to be successful. Students want teachers who care about them, but they also want teachers who are effective and at the top of their game in the classroom.

What Is an Effective Teacher?

Goe, Bell, and Little (2008) provide the watershed amplification of "effective teachers," examining the themes consistently found to be true in the research:

1 Effective teachers have high expectations for all students and help students learn, as measured by value-added or other test-based growth measures or by alternative measures.
2 Effective teachers contribute to positive academic, attitudinal, and social outcomes for students such as regular attendance, on-time promotion to the next grade, on-time graduation, self-efficacy, and cooperative behavior.
3 Effective teachers use diverse resources to plan and structure engaging learning opportunities; monitor student progress formatively, adapting instruction as needed; and evaluate learning using multiple sources of evidence.
4 Effective teachers contribute to the development of classrooms and schools that value diversity and civic-mindedness.

5 Effective teachers collaborate with other teachers, administrators, parents and education professionals to ensure student success, particularly the success of students with special needs and those at high risk for failure.

(p. 8)

Effective Teaching and Learning in Classrooms

To drill deeper, what would effectiveness in practice look and sound like in the classroom? Effective teachers, according to Bullmaster-Day (2011), "follow a regular instructional cycle. They assess student learning; analyze assessment results to identify student strengths and needs; plan and implement instruction based on identified strengths and needs; and monitor student progress to further adjust instruction as needed" (p. 4). Effective teachers demonstrate high levels of teaching expertise, meet accountability standards, and share professional knowledge with their colleagues (Hunt, Wiseman, & Touzel, 2009). Effective teachers care deeply about students and their success (Wright, Horn, & Sanders, 1997), and they "absolutely, unequivocally, make a difference in student learning" (Stronge & Tucker, 2000, p. 1).

Teacher evaluation systems are built around teacher performance standards and the instructional practices that give life to the standards and support the assessment of teaching. To see this relationship, teacher evaluation frameworks are examined.

Teacher Evaluation Frameworks— Connections to Effective Teaching

Researchers have developed rigorous teacher evaluation frameworks and accompanying rubrics (Ingvarson, 2002). Danielson's (1996) Framework for Teaching, the Bill and Melinda Gates Foundation's (2010) Measures of Effective Teaching Project, and Marzano's (2013) Causal Teacher Evaluation Model are well-known examples of such frameworks. These frameworks have been extensively applied in various teacher evaluation systems to assess teacher performance.

Domains Within Frameworks

Teacher evaluation frameworks are built around domains (Danielson, 1996; Marzano, 2013), standards (Stronge, 2010), or measures (Bill & Melinda Gates Foundation, 2013). Although there are differences, the frameworks are built on the research about teacher effectiveness. The domains capture performance areas associated with instructional and other classroom practices and some include dispositions of effective teachers. The following capture the most salient points related to teacher effectiveness as found in teacher evaluation systems.

Subject Matter Knowledge

A fundamental element that contributes to student learning and achievement is a teacher's knowledge of subject matter (Danielson, 1996; Stronge, 2010) and refers to the amount and organization of knowledge (Shulman, 1986). Subject-matter knowledge is a "teacher's understanding of subject facts, concepts, principles, and the methods through which they are integrated cognitively to determine the teacher's pedagogical thinking and decision making" (Stronge, 2010, p. 19). Researchers believe that an effective teacher addresses the appropriate curriculum standards and integrates key elements and higher-level thinking skills during instruction (Danielson, 1996; Stronge, 2010). Effective teachers have the ability to link present content with past and future learning experiences, demonstrate the skills relevant to the subject areas, and understand the intellectual, social, emotional, and physical development needs of the age groups they teach (Stronge, 2010). Effective teachers understand the evolving nature of subject-matter knowledge, keep abreast of new ideas in their discipline, and can extend the relationship of their discipline to other content areas (Shulman, 1986).

Instructional Planning and Strategies

An effective teacher uses multiple instructional materials, activities, strategies, and assessment techniques to meet students' needs (Stronge, 2010; Tomlinson, 1999, 2010). Effective teachers support cognitive challenge by providing in-depth explanations of academic content and by covering higher-order concepts and skills. Research indicates that instructional strategies have the most proximal relation to student learning (Marzano, Frontier, & Livingston, 2011; Walberg, 1984).

Marzano et al. (2011) conducted more than 300 experimental and control studies to investigate the relationship of instructional strategies to student achievement. The average effect size for strategies addressed in the studies was 0.42 and, on average, when teachers used certain classroom strategies and displayed certain behaviors, their typical student achievement increased by 16 percentile points. Various other studies found similar results (Tomlinson, 1999; Walberg, 1984).

Assessment

Assessment for learning is a process of evaluating student performance whereby the teacher gathers, analyzes, and uses data to measure learners' progress (Stronge, 2010). Student assessment provides an overview of what the teacher has taught students. Assessment provides

- diagnostic information regarding students' readiness for learning new content;
- formative and summative information needed to monitor student progress;
- motivation for students to stay engaged in their learning; and
- support for students in their own efforts to retain what they have learned.

(Sanders, 2000)

Stronge (2010) indicates that effective teachers use assessment data to develop expectations for students, use a variety of formal and informal assessment strategies, collect and maintain records of student assessment, and develop tools that help students assess their own learning needs.

Learning Environment

Effective teachers create an environment of respect and rapport in their classrooms by the ways they interact with students and by the interactions they encourage and cultivate among students (Danielson, 1996). Effective teachers focus on the organization of learning activities throughout teaching and learning, use instructional time wisely, assume responsibility for student learning, and establish rapport and trustworthiness with students by being fair, caring, and respectful (Marzano, Pickering, & McTighe, 1993). Research indicates that in a positive learning environment, teachers develop an inviting classroom space, have materials and resources ready, and establish classroom rules and procedures (Evertson, 1985; Stronge, 2007). Effective teachers have less disruptive student behaviors than do less effective teachers (Stronge, Ward, Tucker, & Hindman, 2008).

Effective Communication

The ability to communicate is a requisite for teacher effectiveness (Fullan, 1993). Communication is an ability to (1) package and deliver content meaningfully, (2) create an engaging class culture, (3) be sensitive to individual student needs, and (4) connect with the student first as a person and then as a learner (Cornett-DeVito & Worley, 2005).

Contextualizing System Perspectives on Teacher Effectiveness and Effective Teaching

At the heart of any teacher evaluation system are the formative processes such as classroom observations regardless of whether these observations are formal and announced (pre-observation conference, observation, and post-observation conference) or informal and unannounced (classroom observation and post-observation conference). Several questions come to mind about teacher effectiveness in the classroom, especially since teacher effectiveness is related to gains in student achievement. So what does a school leader focus attention on during classroom observations to ensure that teachers are effectively teaching? What do teachers do to ensure that students are learning? What do teachers and leaders need to commit time, energy, and focus to ensure that teaching is student-centric?

Committing to Effective Teaching

In the Clarke County School District (CCSD) in Athens, GA, the Commitments for High Student Performance and the observable practices are those that the system embraces and believes to have a positive impact on student achievement. These Commitments and observable practices have evolved over time, starting in 2009–10 with a series of non-negotiable practices that focused on accountability in a performance-based environment. The CCSD has evolved in its understandings and applications of practices that support student learning through the work of the entire system led by a superintendent, Dr. Philip Lanoue, who focuses much of his time providing system-wide conditions that promote student success.

There are many *observable*, high-yield practices that can help principals recognize effective teaching when they see it. Table 3.1 outlines the document Commitments for High Student Performance developed by the CCSD and the observable practices developed by Zepeda (2014) to reflect the district performance standards. A robust research base supports the observable practices. Examining the research base was also part of the process in developing the Commitments and observable practices. Equally important was the effort and energy around culling practices across and beyond the school system.

Conversations and Involvement as Process Guides

The CCSD engaged teachers, leaders, College of Education faculty at the University of Georgia, and other internal and external community stakeholders in developing the Commitments. Each school and group followed a protocol to ensure conversations focused on giving input, providing possible Commitments to add or delete, editing the words on the page, and so on. Feedback mechanisms were built into the process so insights could be shared every time the document was changed throughout the year-long process. Another step in the process was sending out the final draft of the document to all who had a hand in developing the Commitments for High Student Performance. An overwhelming majority of the teachers in addition to the school leaders endorsed the Commitments to students.

The Question That Guided the Work

Through the process, teachers and leaders vetted the draft Commitments and asked a defining question: What would the observable practice look and sound like in the classroom? A unique feature of the Commitments is that some take into account the work teachers do outside of the classroom. For example, the commitment Planning Practices and its elements would primarily be observed by a leader during a team or grade-level meeting; however, performance in the classroom would undoubtedly be affected if a teacher did not plan.

The observable practices will continue to evolve to keep pace with advances in the research on teaching and learning and from the lessons that CCSD learns from their school improvement efforts. The CCSD believes that high-yield instructional strategies need to be implemented with fidelity in every classroom every day regardless of the content area or grade level.

System-Wide Focus

The observable practices are meant to serve as a guide for teachers and leaders to focus on two major questions:

1   Are students actively engaged in learning?
2   What data—formative and summative—are being examined?

Teaching in a standards-based classroom is not about the teacher as much as it is about the students and how they respond to the teacher, the work, and the variables that can either enhance or detract from teaching and learning. The observable practices can be used to

1   assist teachers in building content knowledge and help teachers increase their understanding of instructional strategies that support its delivery;
2   identify individual and collective strengths as well as the professional learning opportunities needed to sustain and to extend strategies that yield increases in student growth and development;
3   identify collective areas in need of improvement as well as the professional learning opportunities needed to overcome these gaps;

4 unify the efforts of principals, assistant principals, department chairs, and system-level support personnel who engage in announced and unannounced classroom observations;

5 examine targets in the system-wide and site-level school improvement plans;

6 develop and sustain a common lexicon surrounding teaching, learning, instructional strategies, and classroom procedures;

7 provide coherence at the site and system level as it continues to evolve in its understanding about teaching and learning, so that initiatives can be introduced that are focused on the needs of the system (e.g., peer coaching, peer observations, walkthroughs);

8 guide and frame conversations between teachers and leaders; and

9 examine professional learning needs across the system.

(Zepeda, 2014)

Table 3.1 includes the CCSD's Commitments for High Student Performance and the observable practices.

These Commitments have shaped the conversations about teacher performance and effectiveness in the CCSD. The system has been able to drill even deeper in their understandings and conversations because school leaders have tools to help them focus attention on assessing what they see in practice. One such tool is the rubric to accompany the Commitments for High Student Performance (Zepeda, 2015).

Table 3.1 Clarke County School District—Commitments for High Student Performance

Commitment: Professional Knowledge

Element: Professional knowledge is enhanced through appropriate professional development.

Observable Practices
- Through self-assessment, teachers target an area of growth among the performance standards.
- Teachers plan and develop with their evaluator professional development goal(s).
- Teachers and evaluators monitor attainment of professional learning goal(s) throughout the year.

Commitment: Instructional Planning

Element: Dedicate time for collaborative planning to create authentic lessons that align with the required curriculum and provide enrichment opportunities.

Observable Practices
- Teachers collaborate and work in teams to plan lessons.

- Teachers engage in reflective and sustained discussions about the effectiveness of their collaboration.
- Teacher teams collect, interpret, and track data to make decisions related to activities, processes, and procedures for instruction.
- Teachers use digital collaborative planning tools to plan lessons.
- Teachers use digital collaborative tools to create and to engage in ongoing conversation about a unit of study.
- Teachers use a digital collaborative template to analyze student data.

Element: Create lessons using the CCSD Instructional Framework that are engaging, rigorous and aligned to the required curriculum.

Observable Practices

Lesson Plan Structure:

- International Baccalaureate components are part of lesson plans (middle and high schools).
- Lesson plans explicitly list components of the CCSD Instructional Framework (lessons include opening, mini-lesson, work session, and closing) and give specific details about each component:

Beginning of Lesson:

- Establishes the expected learning outcomes.
- Communicates an essential question and/or other type of organizer.
- Connects the previous lesson and/or prerequisite knowledge to new learning.
- Includes activating strategies centered on the standard, element(s), and/or essential question.

Mini-lesson:

- Contains modeling while referencing standards and key vocabulary.
- Includes exemplars (examples of student work that meets or exceeds the standard).

Work Session:

- Students are given time to practice the new content and/or elements of standards by demonstrating relevant, real-world applications.

Closing of Lesson:

- Confirm conceptual understanding by linking back to the opening and the targeted standard or elements as well as the essential question and/or other organizer.
- Students are given time at the end of each lesson to give and receive feedback, clarify understandings, and summarize what was learned.

Engagement:

- Lessons incorporate content in which the standards promote higher-order thinking, problem-posing tasks, and/or problem-solving tasks.
- Prior data (e.g., standardized test scores, quizzes, etc.) are used to plan for instruction, instructional methods, and the resources needed.
- Flexible groups are used for students in need of additional and/or different forms of instruction.
- Teachers create lessons which contain sections that can be archived and accessible 24/7 for review, remediation, and extension by students and families.

Element: Use assessment data to identify learning needs and plan differentiated lessons.

Observable Practices

- Teachers and teams develop lesson plans that reflect differentiation based on data, needs, and/or standards.
- The rigor within assessment items equals the depth of the knowledge level of the standard it measures.
- Assessment data are used to adapt a lesson or strategy if instruction is not working for a student, or to offer new challenges for students who have mastered curriculum.
- Prior data (e.g., standardized test scores, quizzes, etc.) are used to plan for instruction, instructional methods, and the resources needed.
- Teachers disaggregate assessment data using digital tools.
- Teachers gather and archive samples of student work to use as exemplars.

Commitment: Instructional Strategies

Element: Facilitate instruction so that students make connections between prior learning and new learning.

Observable Practices

- A variety of resources are used to make connections across disciplines.
- The creation of new insights and new relationships between ideas is supported.
- Prior knowledge is purposely activated.
- Students guide their own learning as they
  - make decisions about their work;
  - assemble an end product; and/or
  - engage in self-assessment through the use of rubrics, process journals, etc.
- Instructional practices incorporate personalized learning in which student interest is piqued to encourage ownership of learning.
- Students use digital tools to connect prior learning to new learning in any of the following ways:
  - Participate in collaborative conversations.
  - Create a common space where students share information.
  - Engage in digital media (i.e., videos, podcasts, screencasts, etc.) to connect to prior knowledge.
  - Access multiple digital resources.
- Students use digital portfolios to create work across disciplines and/or years as a way to make connections to prior learning.
- The teacher uses activating strategies centered on the standard(s), element(s), and essential question (opening).
- Instruction ends with a summary activity that assesses student understanding of the standards/elements (closing).

Element: Provide opportunities for each student to use globally diverse perspectives in seeking solutions to meaningful problems.

Observable Practices

- Teachers present lessons around a particular question or problem.
- Teachers relate learning to real-world situations.
- Teachers use questioning strategies to promote higher-order thinking.
- Teachers and students extend learning with problem-solving situations.
- Students identify perspectives that may offer unique insights, responses, and solutions.
- Students use digital tools to communicate with people in different parts of the world to discuss current topics.

Element: Use digital media to support student learning.

Observable Practices

- Students make connections between prior learning and new learning through the use of digital tools.
- When seeking solutions to meaningful problems, students use digital tools to obtain globally diverse perspectives.
- Teachers ensure that assessments and performance-based tasks are designed, administered, and/or summarized using digital tools.
- Teachers use digital tools to provide frequent and meaningful feedback on student work.
- Teachers use digital tools to allow students to act as decision makers and to take responsibility for their own learning.
- Teachers use digital tools to differentiate the content, process(es), and/or product(s) of instruction.

Commitment: Differentiated Instruction

Element: Differentiate instruction so that every student is challenged.

Observable Practices

Teachers differentiate content, process, and/or product in any of the following ways:

Differentiated Content:

- Teachers re-teach an idea or skill in small group to struggling learners.
- Teachers extend, enrich, and/or accelerate thinking or skills of advanced learners.
- Teachers offer multiple modes of learning to encourage student engagement.
- Teachers provide students with choice in the complexity of content so they can select learning tasks that match their level of understanding.
- Teachers present content in incremental steps to scaffold learning.
- Students use digital tools and digital media to scaffold and/or to accelerate content.

Differentiated Process:

- Teachers use varied instructional strategies and activities for students.
- Teachers monitor and pace instruction based on data that identifies the individual needs of students.
- Teachers use a variety of grouping strategies and instructional techniques (individual, small group, whole group).
- Teachers use specific and varied digital tools based on individual student needs.
- Students are either assigned or are able to choose digital tools according to their learning styles to demonstrate learning.

Differentiated Product:

- Teachers use kinesthetic, hands-on learning opportunities that encourage students to produce their own products.
- Teachers allow students to work alone or in small groups on projects and performance tasks.
- Teachers give students choices or menus with a variety of end-product options.

Commitment: Assessment Strategies

Element: Communicate rigorous expectations for mastery of the required curriculum.

Observable Practices

- Teachers ensure that standards are addressed in the lesson using language that students can understand and master.

- Teachers provide multiple opportunities for students to show mastery across a variety of modalities.
- Students are involved in identifying strategies to increase their learning and take responsibility for their own learning.
- Teachers showcase student exemplars in a digital environment.
- Teachers and/or students use digital rubrics when evaluating mastery of standards.

Element: Provide frequent and meaningful feedback on student work.

Observable Practices

- Teachers give specific feedback and provide opportunities for students to extend, rephrase, and/or apply the skills and knowledge of the standards.
- Teachers use rubrics to provide criteria against which students can assess and compare their learning.
- Students provide oral or written feedback to self-assess or provide peer feedback on the learning objective or learning criteria.
- Students participate in brief and focused digital assessments that provide specific feedback on misconceptions or successes.
- Feedback is provided to students through digital tools, and the feedback is incorporated into student portfolios.
- Students use digital tools to monitor and to assess their own work, peer work, or that of exemplars.
- Teachers and students are able to monitor changes that students make to their work using digital tools.

Commitment: Assessment Uses

Element: Use a variety of assessments and performance-based tasks to design, monitor, assess, and adjust instruction to support student learning.

Observable Practices

- Teachers adjust their instruction during class based on "minute-by-minute" assessments that give students immediate feedback.
- Teachers give descriptive feedback to students as they engage in activities, in class discussions, etc.
- Students are involved in the self-assessment of their own learning.
- Students use digital tools in the classroom to submit assessment answers, review assessment feedback, and reflect on assessment feedback.
- Teachers use digital tools in the classroom to capture student responses from assessment items, provide feedback, and modify instructional strategies or approach.

Commitment: Positive Learning Environment

Element: Respect the individuality of each student and support academic growth, social emotional development, and physical well-being.

Observable Practices

- Teachers establish routines and rituals to ensure time and classroom space promote student engagement.
- Teachers model expected student behaviors.
- Teachers provide care and concern for student social-emotional and physical well-being in the classroom.
- Instruction and room arrangements support grouping patterns that address not only intellectual needs but also the social, emotional, and physical needs of students.
- Teachers support the health of children through collaboration with external agencies.

Commitment: Academically Challenging Environment

Element: Create a learning environment in which students are decision makers and take responsibility for their own learning.

Observable Practices
- Teachers set high expectations and provide support to achieve expectations.
- Students have some degree of choice regarding methods of learning.
- Students control aspects of the digital media according to their individual learning styles and needs (i.e., color text and background variation for dyslexia, fewer choices, word banks, etc.).
- Students receive individualized feedback based on achievement and/or performance assessment.
- Students are self-reflective and can articulate their strengths and weaknesses and progress toward meeting the standard.

Commitment: Professionalism

Element: Collaborate with communities to enhance and promote student learning.

Observable Practices
- Teachers are aware of additional services, resources, and supports within the school and community.
- Teachers forge relationships with community members and/or resources that add value to the educational experience for students.
- Teachers enhance connections between schools and communities through the use of digital tools.

Element: Involve stakeholders in identifying school needs and developing solutions.

Observable Practices
- Student learning is promoted through conferencing and other outreach efforts between teachers and parents.
- Parents are involved in problem solving by sharing their insights related to the situation.
- Teachers are proactive in developing solutions to problems in a timely manner.

Element: Exhibit professional and ethical conduct at all times.

Observable Practices
- Teachers model excellent attendance, demeanor, and composure.
- Teachers follow district, state, and school-level policies regarding duties and responsibilities.

Commitment: Communication

Element: Establish partnerships with families through open, frequent, and meaningful collaboration.

Observable Practices
- Teachers support a safe, comfortable, accessible, and welcoming environment for parents and guardians.
- Teachers offer parallel support for students and their families by working alongside afterschool program personnel.
- Teachers are involved in ongoing, two-way communication with parents throughout the year.

45

- Parents are invited to participate in learning activities in and out of the classroom.
- Teachers initiate communication with families via email or other digital tools.
- Teachers use digital tools to allow parents to understand the curriculum and expectations for student performance.
- Teachers use Google Hangout to have parents "visit" or participate in classroom presentations.

Element: Respect the diversity of all stakeholders.

Observable Practices
- Teachers model respect and acceptance through interactions and outreach with families and other stakeholders.
- Teachers create an affirming attitude toward students from culturally diverse backgrounds by learning about students and adopting culturally responsive teaching and communication practices.
- Teachers forge purposeful connections with programs for culturally diverse populations within the school (e.g., families), external stakeholders, and organizations.

Commitments for High Student Performance used with permission of the Clarke County School District; Observable Practices from Zepeda, 2014

Rubrics

Rubrics support both teachers and leaders in being able to assess levels of performance. The CCSD rubric accompanying the observable practices associated with the Commitments for High Student Performance drive four very important processes:

1   teacher self-assessment and reflection on practices;
2   assessment made throughout the year during classroom observations, examination of student work, and so forth;
3   guiding the conversations; and
4   pinpointing areas for targeted professional development.

Table 3.2 provides a snapshot of the rubric developed to illustrate the performance levels related to the observable practices (Zepeda, 2015). Following the format of the Georgia Teacher Keys Effectiveness System (TKES), the rubric lays out four levels of performance, from lowest (Level I) to highest (Level IV).

Examine the key wording that separates the performance levels:

- Level I   = rarely
- Level II   = inconsistently
- Level III = consistently
- Level IV   = continually

Table 3.2 CCSD Rubric—Differentiated Instruction Commitment

PERFORMANCE STANDARD 4: Differentiated Instruction Commitment The teacher challenges and supports each student by differentiating instruction, content, and matching resources based on individual student needs and skills.			
Level IV	**Level III**	**Level II**	**Level I**
The teacher continually challenges students through varying methods to differentiate instruction, content, and digital resources to extend, enrich, and/or accelerate learning.	The teacher consistently challenges students through varying methods to differentiate instruction, content, and digital resources to extend, enrich, and/or accelerate learning.	The teacher inconsistently challenges students through varying methods to differentiate instruction, content, and digital resources to extend, enrich, and/or accelerate learning.	The teacher rarely challenges students through varying methods to differentiate instruction, content, and digital resources to extend, enrich, and/or accelerate learning.

Used with permission of the Clarke County School District (Zepeda, 2015)

When observing a teacher or giving feedback about practice, both teachers and leaders need to be explicit about the differences in the key words that align with performance levels. Through conversations over time, practice applying the rubric, and professional development, leaders become more familiar and confident in discerning the performance differences between levels. The conversations between teachers and leaders will support the development of a common language to discuss observable practices and corresponding performance. In many ways, performance, regardless of level, needs to be the focus of conversations. With observable practices as a guide, the discussions will naturally become more focused. The observable practices presented are not inclusive in that there are many other practices that could support the Commitments for High Student Performance.

The reader is encouraged to revisit the image of his or her best and worst teacher and then think of the descriptions offered in Chapter 1 to illustrate the ranges in teacher performance. Reflect on the performance levels of the teachers in your own building. Any effective teacher evaluation system focuses on teaching and teacher effectiveness: This is what the leader must be able to recognize in practice; then he or she must be able to discern the gamut of ratings from unsatisfactory to exemplary.

References

Bill & Melinda Gates Foundation. (2010). *Working with teachers to develop fair and reliable measures of effective teaching.* Seattle: Author. Retrieved from http://www.metproject.org/downloads/met-framing-paper.pdf

Bill & Melinda Gates Foundation. (2013). *Ensuring fair and reliable measures of effective teaching: Culminating findings from the MET project's three-year study.* Seattle: Author. Retrieved from http://www.metproject.org/downloads/MET_Ensuring_Fair_and_Reliable_Measures_Practitioner_Brief.pdf

Bridgeland, J. M., Dilulio, J. J., Jr., & Morrison, K. B. (2006). *The silent epidemic: Perspectives of high school drop outs.* Washington, D.C.: Civic Enterprises in Association with Peter D. Hart Research Associates, Bill & Melinda Gates Foundation. Retrieved from https://docs.gatesfoundation.org/Documents/TheSilentEpidemic3-06Final.pdf

Bullmaster-Day, M. L. (2011). *Let the learner do the learning: What we know about effective teaching.* New York: Touro College, Lander Center for Educational Research. Retrieved from http://gse.touro.edu/research--outreach/resources--development/literature-reviews

Cornett-DeVito, M. M., & Worley, D. W. (2005). A front row seat: A phenomenological investigation of learning disabilities. *Communication Education, 54*(4), 312–333. doi: 10.1080/03634520500442178

Danielson, C. (1996). *The framework for professional practice*. Alexandria, VA: Association for Supervision and Curriculum Development.

Evertson, C. M. (1985). Training teachers in classroom management: An experimental study in secondary school classrooms. *The Journal of Educational Research, 79*(1), 51–58. Retrieved from http://www.tandfonline.com/loi/vjer20#.VaFKIvnvmPl

Fullan, M. G. (1993). Why teachers must become change agents. *Educational Leadership, 50*(6), 12–17. Retrieved from http://www.csus.edu/indiv/j/jelinekd/EDTE%20227/Fullen%20change.pdf

Goe, L., Bell, C., & Little, O. (2008). *Approaches to evaluating teacher effectiveness: A research synthesis*. Washington, D.C.: National Comprehensive Center for Teacher Quality. Retrieved from http://files.eric.ed.gov/fulltext/ED521228.pdf

Hunt, G. H., Wiseman, D. G., & Touzel, T. J. (2009). *Effective teaching: Preparation and Implementation* (4th ed.). Springfield, IL: Charles C Thomas.

Ingvarson, L. (2002). Development of a national standards framework for the teaching profession. *Australian Council for Educational Research,* (1), 1–32. Retrieved from http://research.acer.edu.au/teaching_standards/7

Marzano, R. J. (2013). *The Marzano teacher evaluation model*. Englewood, CO: Marzano Research Laboratory. Retrieved from www.marzanoresearch.com

Marzano, R. J., Frontier, T., & Livingston, D. (2011). *Effective supervision: Supporting the art and science of teaching*. Alexandria, VA: Association for Supervision and Curriculum Development.

Marzano, R. J., Pickering, D., & McTighe, J. (1993). *Assessing student outcomes: Performance assessment using the dimensions of learning model*. Alexandria, VA: Association for Supervision and Curriculum Development. Retrieved from http://eric.ed.gov/?id=ED461665

Noguera, P., & Wing, J. Y. (Eds.) (2006). *Unfinished business: Closing the racial and achievement gap in our schools*. San Francisco: Jossey-Bass.

Sanders, W. L. (2000). Value-added assessment from student achievement data: Opportunities and hurdles. *Journal of Personnel Evaluation in Education, 14*(4), 329–339. Retrieved from http://link.springer.com/article/10.1023%2FA%3A1013008006096

Shulman, L. S. (1986). Those who understand: Knowledge growth in teaching. *Journal of Education, 15*(2), 4–14. Retrieved from http://www.bu.edu/sed/about-us/journal-of-education

Stronge. J. H. (2007). *Qualities of effective teachers*. Alexandria, VA: Association for Supervision and Curriculum Development.

Stronge, J. H. (2010). *Effective teachers = student achievement: What the research says*. Larchmont, NY: Eye on Education.

Stronge, J. H., & Tucker, P. D. (2000). *Teacher evaluation and student achievement*. Washington, D.C.: National Education Association.

Stronge, J. H., Ward, T. J., Tucker, P.D., & Hindman, J. L. (2008). What is the relationship between teacher quality and student achievement? An exploratory study. *Journal of Personnel Evaluation in Education, 20(3–4),* 165–184. doi: 10.1007/s11092-008-9053-z

Tomlinson, C. A. (1999). Mapping a route toward differentiated instruction. *Educational Leadership, 57*(1), 12–17. Retrieved from http://www.ascd.org/ASCD/pdf/journals/ed_lead/el199909_tomlinson.pdf

Tomlinson, C. A. (2010). Learning to love assessment. *Educational Leadership, 65*(4), 8–13. Retrieved from http://www.ascd.org/publications/educational-leadership.aspx

Walberg, H. J. (1984). Improving the productivity of America's schools. *Educational Leadership, 41*(8), 19–27. Retrieved from http://www.ascd.org/ASCD/pdf/journals/ed_lead/el_198405_walberg.pdf

Wright, S. P., Horn, S. P., & Sanders, W. L. (1997). Teachers and classroom context effects on student achievement: Implications for teacher evaluation. *Journal of Personnel Evaluation in Education, 11*(1), 57–67. doi:10.1023/A:1007999204543

Zepeda, S. J. (2014). *Fidelity report: CCSD commitments for high student performance.* Presentation to the CCSD Board of Education. Athens, GA: Clarke County School District.

Zepeda, S. J. (2015). *CCSD teacher evaluation rubric aligned to the Teacher Keys Effectiveness System.* Athens, GA: Clarke County School District.

4 Underperforming Teachers In and Out of the Classroom

There are no universal definitions for an underperforming teacher and no universally accepted ways to support the needs of teachers whose performance in or out of the classroom is less than stellar. The professional literature and research has not painted a positive image of underperforming teachers; moreover, underperforming teachers have not escaped attention from the media, with the bantering of such terms as "bad apples" or the notorious NFL draft handing off underperforming teachers or doing the "dance of the lemons" (Bolch, 2015).

Think back to the 1984 movie *Teachers* and the character Mr. Ditto, whose only instructional strategy was engaging students with mimeo worksheets while he slept in the back of the room (Russo & Hiller, 1984). Mr. Ditto's students were trained to be quiet and submissive; the instructional method was the "in and out box" for students to pick up or hand in their mimeographed sheets in clock-like drill fashion. The bell-to-bell time consists of mindless work. In fact, Mr. Ditto dies in the classroom, an incident not discovered until the end of the day. Not many parents would want their child to be in Mr. Ditto's class!

Then there is the 1986 movie *Ferris Bueller's Day Off* (Hughes, 1986). Two characters' immediately come to mind, the pedantic Ben Stein, the nameless economics teacher who incessantly repeats "Anyone, Anyone, Anyone?" a mere second after asking a question. The dean of students was more interested in playing "gotcha" with Ferris Bueller, who skips school to visit the Chicago Art Institute. Ferris and the others are mesmerized and engaged in appreciating and learning about art instead of listening to a nameless teacher repeatedly ask "Anyone?"

These might be extreme examples of underperforming teachers glorified by Hollywood, but teachers like this are in your buildings!

Characteristics of Underperformance

Consider the following sketches of teachers who are experiencing issues.

Teacher A: Mary Chuck, a fifth-year teacher, generally is on her game, but every few months, she has classroom periods during which she needs support to carry forward instruction.

Teacher B: When a supervisor enters the room, the spotlights go on and Barney Wolfe shines for the observation. However, the longer the observer is in the room, the dimmer the lights shine. When he runs out of materials before the end of the class period, Barney assigns students practice problems, stating, "If you talk, then there are a dozen or so problems for homework."

Teacher C: Peter Schmidt keeps law and order in the classroom. He lectures exclusively, delivering a content-rich monologue from bell to bell, with students intermittently reading aloud passages from the textbook. Peter's students have not done well on the state-mandated exams in English. Looking back at the results over the last 3 years, trend data indicate that his students have had the lowest scores in the building.

These brief sketches portray degrees of underperformance and illustrate that there is no one-size portrait of what underperformance looks and sounds like in and out of the classroom. For our purposes, the term *underperforming* is used throughout this book; however, earlier literature and research primarily used the word *marginal* to describe teachers whose performance was less than acceptable. Though there are no concrete definitions, underperforming (marginal) teachers are generally described as those teachers who walk the line between performing well enough to stay employed while under-serving student learning (Zepeda, 2013). Nolan and Hoover (2011) indicate that teachers who underperform "are identified as questionably competent or less than satisfactory in one or more performance-based standards" (p. 296).

Underperformance Inside the Classroom

The underperforming teacher denotes one who does not work up to speed. Recall the Commitments for High Student Performance presented in Chapter 3. These Commitments and the observable practices all pointed to teacher performance and behaviors and the associated practices that lead to increasing student learning and engagement. The practices of underperforming teachers do not lead students down the path of learning, and this is a problem! Given the demands of curricular standards tied to statewide tests and the press for teachers to be effective in supporting increases in student achievement, the classroom is the hub of learning. Smith (2008) tells us that a marginal teacher

- **Does not** maintain consistent instruction from "Bell to Bell."
- **Does not** teach to the curriculum or meet objectives that have been set.
- **Does not** show enthusiasm for student learning, students, and teaching.
- **Does not** cultivate good relationships with students.
- **Does not** exhibit good teaching skills.
- **Does not** organize classroom and lessons.
- **Does not** clearly establish behavioral expectations for students.
- **Does not** have mastery of the content area.
- **Does not** provide useful feedback to students in a timely manner.

(p. 213, emphasis in the original)

When a principal steps into the classroom of an underperforming teacher, he or she might see a variety of behaviors that may not immediately identify that teacher as an underperformer. Part of the problem in identifying an underperforming teacher is that the teacher might be putting on a dog and pony show or might be at a point in the class in which there is competence; alternatively, the observer might not be fully up to speed on what constitutes effective teaching.

The negative indicators of poor teacher performance typically are not isolated to just one area or a single time frame (beginning or ending of class) within a class period as the lesson of the hour unfolds. The school leader needs to have a working knowledge of the subject matter, what good instruction looks and sounds like, what constitutes a positive learning environment, and a host of other areas that keep the teacher and the students focused on learning (see Chapter 3).

Underperformance Outside the Classroom

Often, underperforming teachers have issues that spill out of the classroom. For example, an underperforming teacher might be absent quite often and not leave lesson plans for the substitute teacher. School systems, state departments of education, and the agencies that certify teachers have duties and responsibilities or standard expectations that apply to all educators. Local school systems typically have their own expectations that are held as non-negotiable. In consultation with the Clarke County School District, the following duties and responsibilities were developed (Zepeda, 2011): The professional duties and responsibilities listed in Table 4.1 elaborate the expectations for all classroom teachers.

Causes of Underperforming Teachers

It may be difficult to identify underperforming teachers because they may not have glaring issues in all areas. This difficulty is further compounded by the fact that underperforming teachers may be efficient at performing well during yearly evaluations, masking subpar teaching that occurs from day to day. Underperformance can be detected only if the principal and key school personnel maintain a strong presence in classrooms, conducting frequent formal and informal observations; monitor student achievement data (pre- and post-tests, yearly standardized test results); examine discipline referrals, attendance patterns, parent, student, and teacher complaints; and the like.

Table 4.1 Professional Duties and Responsibilities

1   Reports to work regularly as assigned
Attendance is an essential component of a quality learning experience and therefore, excessive absence and/or tardiness do interfere with the daily operations of the school. Hence, teachers:

- Are on time daily.
- Report to morning duties as assigned and on time.
- Sign in in accordance to building policies and procedures.

2   Provides adequate information, plans, and materials for substitute teachers
Substitute teachers play an integral role in moving the instructional mission forward in the absence of the regularly assigned teacher; therefore, teachers ensure that

- Lesson plans are created and available to the substitute teacher in the event of an unexpected absence.
- Lesson plans provide work and other items for students to not lose instructional time.

3   Enforces school procedures concerning student conduct and discipline
A key indicator in the school effectiveness literature is that orderly environments enhance learning; thus

- Discipline in the classroom, hallways, and other areas of the building is handled in a way in which students learn lessons from infractions.
- The teacher handles discipline and refers students to the office only under extreme conditions.
- The teacher sets an orderly and learning-conducive environment.
- The teacher works cooperatively in the prevention of disruptive behaviors in the classroom.
- The teacher explains classroom rules and regulations early in year, explicating consequences, and fairly and consistently upholds expectations for orderly behavior.
- All certified staff is responsible for corridor control and conduct in accordance with plans developed by the principal.
- Corridor supervision includes supervision of restrooms and other student-used facilities and areas.
- Teachers hold the responsibility for ensuring that every student under the teacher's supervision has left the classroom and sees that facilities are properly secured.
- Teachers do not leave students unattended in the classroom, hallways, etc.

4   Maintains accurate grades to document student performance
Grading is critical to the learning process for both students and teachers. For students, grading clarifies what they understand, what they don't understand, and where they can improve. Grading also provides *feedback to instructors about their students' learning*, and this information can inform future teaching decisions (Walvoord & Anderson, 1998). To this end, teachers

- Keep accurate records detailing student grades.
- Review grades with students, parents, and the principal/supervisor.
- Use the results of tests, quizzes, and other results systematically to refine instruction, make accommodations, etc.

5   Maintains confidentiality regarding student and records information
Schools are data rich and, as such, special care needs to taken to ensure that teachers

- Maintain records in a safe and secure manner.
- Share information with only appropriate school personnel, parents, and legal guardians.

6   Assumes responsibility for professional growth

Teachers are professionals and one way to grow as a professional is to engage in professional development that

- Aligns with personal, school-wide, and system-wide school improvement efforts.
- Promotes learning from others in the school, system, and beyond.
- Aligns with standards-based learning environments.

7   Maintains accurate and complete records and submits as required and on time

Information is critical to the system, and teachers need to be mindful that information is often time-sensitive; therefore, teachers need to

- Maintain accurate and up-to-date records on students and their progress, programs, and the impact on the instructional program, etc.
- Be timely in providing complete and accurate information when requested by the supervisor and/or principal.
- Maintain information and records that are presentable in format.

8   Demonstrates ethical behavior as outlined in the PSC Code of Ethics

Every teacher must be familiar with the Georgia Professional Standards Commission's Code of Ethics.

9   Interacts in a respectful, civil, and professional manner with students, families, staff, and school leaders

Civility, respect, and professional conduct are norms to which the Clarke County School District subscribes; therefore, teachers

- Treat students, parents, administrators, and community members with respect.
- Embrace civility while resolving conflict.
- Show tact when communicating verbally, non-verbally, and in writing with all constituents of the Clarke County School System.

10   Attends and participates in faculty meetings

Faculty meetings are called at the discretion of the principal, and it is an expectation that teachers will

- Attend all faculty meetings.
- Be punctual and stay for the entire meeting.
- Attend to the purposes of the meeting.
- Give their full attention to the meeting process by avoiding using cell phones, laptop computers, and other devices that distract attention from the meeting, its speakers, and small- and large-group work within meetings.

11   Models correct language, oral and written

Communicating is essential, and it is expected that teachers will

- Use proper language;
- Use grammatically correct sentences when speaking and writing; and
- Refrain from using vernacular when communicating with students, parents, colleagues, administrators, and other system stakeholders.

12   Actively supports the school improvement plan

School improvement plans at the building and system levels play a pivotal role—they outline areas in which the system or building or both need to focus attention. Therefore, teachers

- Support the building and system-wide plans of improvement.
- Actively work toward meeting and exceeding school improvement target areas.

- Engage in the work of school improvement in team meetings, department meetings, grade-level meetings, and other working configurations as deemed appropriate by the principal, supervisor, or central office personnel.
- Keep accurate records that support the school or system-wide school improvement plan.
- Participate in team meetings, grade-level meetings, and other meetings associated with school improvement.

13   Establishes relationships with families and community

Schools serve the purpose to educate children whose parents and the community entrust to the care of the Clarke County School District. To this end, teachers are expected to

- Establish relationships with the families, guardians, and other care takers whose children are enrolled in the Clarke County School District.
- Engage in behaviors that signal confidence in the school and its system, and lends credibility to the teacher in his/her role as teacher.

14   Works cooperatively with school district leaders, support personnel, colleagues, and families

The educative process spans beyond the classroom; therefore, teachers

- Cooperate with other colleagues, including special education services, social work services, psychological services, and any other entity within and outside of the system that can positively impact student learning and personal growth.
- Work in concert with grade-level meetings, subject-area meetings, and other meetings.

15   Seeks first to get facts and gain an understanding of a student's situation before making decisions

Students come to school to get an education first, but students often come to school with many factors that could, perhaps, impede learning. To maximize learning, teachers actively

- Seek opportunities to understand students and the situations that encourage or impede learning.
- Treat students in a kind and caring way while making decisions regarding sanctions, etc.
- Exhibit empathy when dealing with students.
- Rely on factual data that are analyzed before making decisions.

16   Additional duties added locally

Used with permission of the Clarke County School District, Athens, GA. Duties and responsibilities developed by Zepeda (2011)

Sources of Evidence

Student learning is the center of all efforts for systems and their teachers and would include, for example, "common statewide standards for teaching" (Darling-Hammond, 2012) as the foundation for anchoring evidence related to student learning. Beyond the single assessment, evidence of student learning would be teacher judgment and numerous other measures and artifacts (Darling-Hammond, 2012). Stiggins (2014) is resolute that "high-quality evidence must

Table 4.2 Data Collection and Evidence

Data collection/method	Evidence
Classroom observations	Notes from formal and informal classroom observations
Parent complaints	Written, phone calls, emails
Student complaints	Written, phone calls, emails
Complaints from teachers, co-teachers, and para-professionals	Written, oral, emails
Observations during team, grade, and subject area meetings	Written notes
Student achievement scores	Test scores, patterns in grade distribution
Student survey results	Scores and open-ended responses
Parent survey results	Scores and open-ended responses
Goal-setting targets	Individual teacher goals, markers of progress, and next steps in the process for developing new goals

be carefully stored, assembled, and presented in a simple and understandable form" (p. 86). Table 4.2 highlights areas in which evidence could be examined while working with teachers.

Repeating History

History is important and past evaluations could give insight into a teacher's present situation. A principal new to the position would find it invaluable to refer to prior assessments of performance, but caution is offered. The principal must be cautious to not be influenced too much by such documentation as past reports and notes in files. The principal can begin to unpack a teacher's background by asking the following five questions:

1   What is the teacher's history in the building and in the district?
2   What do prior reports regarding the teacher's performance indicate?
3   What situation or context has brought the teacher's performance to attention?
4   Have there been any sudden shifts in the school or district environment such as changes in school demographics or a change in the teacher's responsibilities or assignments?

5   What other data can be examined to help understand the context of teachers and their performance?

What Causes Teachers to Underperform?

There is no concrete answer to the question, What causes teachers to underperform? Teachers at any stage of their career can become underperforming. Curriculum and content changes, new standards, assessments, and the like can cause teachers to experience dips in their performance. Not all dips in performance are symptomatic of an underperforming teacher who needs a formalized plan of improvement. The dips associated with changes in content standards, for example, could be tackled through informal means and include discussions with groups of teachers, targeted professional learning, peer coaching, and such. Here are some possible causes of teacher underperformance.

Fuhr (1990) believed that marginal teachers could have issues clustered around

- *lack of training*: teachers who do not grasp basic teaching techniques;
- *personal reasons*: teachers who have serious personal problems that interfere with teaching or perhaps carrying out responsibilities outside of the classroom; and
- *poor attitudes*: teachers who have negative or poor attitudes about teaching, who know what is expected but refuse to do it.

Again, the causes for underperformance will vary case by case. A few more causes are beginning to emerge and include entitlement and issues surrounding generational attitudes and beliefs.

Entitlement—But I Am Deserving...

A look at entitlement might shed some light on underperforming teachers. The literature and research about entitlement have recently begun to focus on the relationship of workplace attitudes and worker beliefs, which is important given the rapid way in which younger people are replacing retiring workers. The trends related to staffing patterns follow logic that a younger teacher replaces a teacher with 30-plus years of experience. Although there is research about entitlement, much of this research has been applied in the business sector and conducted by researchers using psychological constructs to study intergenerational aspects (Foster, 2013; Twenge, Campbell, Hoffman, & Lance, 2010) and organizational behaviors and personality (Zitek, Jordan, Monin, & Leach, 2010).

As high-stakes teacher evaluation systems evolve to attach merit pay to performance, the entitlement mentality could evolve, as witnessed with business-sector pay for performance systems. Entitlement emerges as people always want more, and many who are entitled believe they deserve it. Understanding entitlement can support principals and other supervisory personnel who work with a range of teachers whose behaviors and attitudes might be getting in the way of teaching, working effectively with peers, and fulfilling other obligations including assigned duties and responsibilities.

A sense of entitlement is an attitude and belief that one "deserves special treatment … [a] preferential treatment to get what they want and to act as they want" (Performance Management Consulting, 2013, para. 3). Entitlement stems from many motivations that might include "longevity, seniority, credentials, past performance …even overly healthy egos [and] superiority" (Performance Management Consulting, 2013, para. 7). Also, when people feel as if they have been victimized, there could be a sense of "you owe me" (Zitek et al., 2010) as a way of compensating from the belief of being wronged.

Drilling Deeper in Practice

> Ms. Ortega applied for the department chair position and was not chosen. Subsequently, the principal who supervises Ms. Ortega notes that her classroom performance has started to slump; activities are scattered, lessons do not match curricular guidelines, and students are engaged in off-task behaviors. During a conversation between the principal and the teacher, Ms. Ortega shares that she deserved to get the position because she had more seniority than the teacher chosen for the department head position and she had "paid her dues."

Takeaways

When underperformance is pointed out, Ms. Ortega assumes a victim stance, believing that she was wronged. Ms. Ortega's underperformance must be addressed according to what was observed in the classroom, leaving the smoke-cloud of not getting the department head position off the table. Ms. Ortega believes she was entitled to the department head position. The principal's work is to find out what is motivating Ms. Ortega so you can act accordingly.

Related to teaching, professionalism and entitlement are at opposite ends of the spectrum. Foster (2013) identifies behaviors and attitudes that are manifested in entitlement and are worth examining in relation to underperformance. Table 4.3 provides an overview of possible manifestation behaviors of underperforming teachers who believe they are entitled.

Table 4.3 Attitudes of Entitlement and Behaviors of Underperforming Teachers

Entitlement attitudes	Possible behaviors of underperforming teachers
Selfish behaviors	Unwilling to share with fellow teachers, students, and the community that the school serves
No sense of fairness	Excessive complaints
Resistant	Refuses to adopt and adapt lessons and other materials related to new standards, information gained from examining student work
Withdrawn from work	Attends meetings but does not participate in discussions; comes to meetings late or skips meetings; absent
Disenchanted	Disappointed with leadership, students, or policies or procedures
9-to-5 mentality	Comes in at the last minute before sign-in; is at the door waiting for the last bus to leave the parking lot
Rigid boundaries between work and home; the mantra "work is not life"	Does little to prepare for classes from one day to the next after hours.
Does not contribute; lacks the motivation to do the heavy lifting to get the work done	Sits back and lets others do the work; hides in the team; does not volunteer to take the lead on tasks
Does not have to work for success	Skates by using materials developed by other teachers, relies on pre-packaged instructional materials
Wants more than he or she deserves	Takes the credit for accomplishments of the team; wants extra time allotted to complete tasks with tight deadlines

Adapted from Foster (2013)

A Generational Thing

Now it's time to focus on some attitudes and beliefs that might be generational (Foster, 2013; Twenge et al., 2010). Here are some considerations for looking at the "generational" patterns that could be at play in your building. Thinking about generational differences is important because teachers who retire will more than likely be replaced with younger teachers. Optimally, teachers work with one another collaboratively such that everyone in the group contributes to building a learning environment focused on student growth.

Given the complexities of curriculum, the development of numerous assessments, the work needed to deliver the curriculum effectively with varied instructional methods, and the proliferation of co-teaching, for example, it is important to be aware of the ways in which different generations *might* work individually and collectively in teams. Table 4.4 gives some highlights of generational attitudes. However, the reader is cautioned *not* to make

Table 4.4 Generational Attitudes

Generation	Year markers	Description/work habits
Silent Generation	1925–1945	• Seek structure • Build relationships with coworkers • Loyal to the company • Achieving the goals of the organization
Baby Boomers	1946–1964	• Results-driven • Idealistic • Willing to put in the time needed to get done whatever work needs to be completed on time
Generation X (Gen X)	1965–1981	• Individualistic and self-focused—often referred to as the *me generation* • Multitask • Lack focus • Busy checking emails • Text-messaging • Making careless errors
Generation Y (Gen Me, Gen X, Millennials, nGen, iGen); also known as the *entitlement generation*	1982–1999	• Individualistic and self-focused—often referred to as the *me generation* • Believe they are owed certain rights and benefits without earning them—instant gratification • Lack personal accountability • Inflated sense of self

Adapted from Bauerlein, (2013); Campbell, Bonacci, Shelton, Exline, & Bushman, (2004); "entitlement generation," (n.d.); Rourke, (2011); Twenge et al. (2010)

generalizations, because there are many differing points of view, and there is no way that a list can include all factors influencing how or why a generation performs as it does in the workforce.

Coggshall, Behrstock-Sherratt, and Drill (2011) analyzed various reports and findings from past research and provided the following insights from their work:

- Gen Y teachers tend to desire more frequent feedback on their teaching and impact from peers, mentors, and principals than do their more veteran colleagues.
- Gen Y teachers tend to be more open to, and have more experience with, shared practice than do their more experienced colleagues.
- Gen Y teachers tend to desire differentiation in rewards and sanctions for themselves and their colleagues based on effort and performance.
- Gen Y teachers want to be evaluated but tend to be very concerned about equity and validity in teacher evaluation.
- Gen Y teachers tend to be very enthusiastic about instructional and social networking technology but expect more from technology than what many schools can deliver.

(p. 6)

Given these insights, Coggshall et al. (2011) make the following recommendations for workplaces:

- Ensure teachers receive regular feedback on their effectiveness.
- Support peer learning and shared practice.
- Recognize (and reward) high performance.
- Have fair, rigorous, and meaningful evaluation systems.
- Leverage technology intelligently to enhance performance.

(p. 2)

Demographic Trends

Teacher experience ranges from the novice to the veteran with discernible patterns that shift over time. Earlier, we looked at adult learning and the relationship to differentiated and developmental types of support (see Chapter 2). Based on a follow-up survey of a nationally representative sample of 4,400 current or former public school teachers in the United States, Goldring, Taie, and Riddles (2014) found that

- Of the 3,377,900 public school teachers who were teaching during the 2011–12 school year, 84 percent remained at the same school ("stayers"), 8 percent moved to a different school ("movers"), and 8 percent left the profession ("leavers") during the following year.
- Among public school teachers with 1–3 years of experience, 80 percent stayed in their base-year school, 13 percent moved to another school, and 7 percent left teaching in 2012–13.
- Among public school teacher movers, 59 percent moved from one public school to another public school in the same district, 38 percent moved from one public school district to another public school district, and 3 percent moved from a public school to a private school between 2011–12 and 2012–13.
- About 30 percent of public school teacher movers changed schools involuntarily in 2012–13.
- About 10 percent of public school teacher leavers left teaching involuntarily in 2012–13.
- About 8 percent of public school teachers who left teaching in 2012–13 were working in an occupation outside the field of education, including military service.
- About 51 percent of public school teachers who left teaching in 2012–13 reported that the manageability of their work load was better in their current position than in teaching.
- Additionally, 53 percent of public school leavers reported that their general work conditions were better in their current position than in teaching.

(Goldring et al., 2014, p. 3)

The big takeaways from these data are (1) 53% of teachers left from year 1 to year 2 in the systems in which they worked, (2) far too many teachers moved from one school or system to another, and (3) 10% of the surveyed teachers left their positions involuntarily.

Ingersoll and Merrill (2010) and Ingersoll, Merrill, and Stuckey (2014) cue readers to some demographic trends that could influence the types of support needed for teachers. By examining the faculty globally and then determining whether there are any patterns, school leaders can be more efficient in pooling talent to support the development and implementation of possible strategies for teachers experiencing like issues. Table 4.5 provides an overview of demographic trends.

Table 4.5 Overview of Demographic Trends

Trend	Description
Ballooning	Student enrollment increases necessitate teacher hiring.
Graying	The age of teachers increases.
Greening	There is an exponentially high number of "new" teachers with fewer "graying" or midcareer teachers to serve as mentors.
Female-dominated	More women than men are teaching, and women continue to enter the field in higher numbers than men.
Less stability	High numbers of teachers leave the profession, causing turnover.
Academic abilities	Teacher academic preparation, the quality of the institution, and other variables such as gender and subject area show variability in teacher quality.

Adapted from Ingersoll and Merrill (2010); Ingersoll, Merrill, and Stuckey (2014)

It is not uncommon for schools to have a disproportionate number of newer and then more veteran teachers. There is a mass of teachers in the middle stages of their careers. All teachers, regardless of experience, need support if they are underperforming in or out of the classroom. The real focus is for school leaders to work with underperforming teachers using formal and informal structures. The ultimate goal is to support the capacity of teachers by improving the quality of teaching. Such improvements will not be forthcoming unless there are focused interventions coupled with feedback that is detailed, with explicit performance improvement targets.

The Leader's Response to Underperforming Teachers

Bridges (1992) indicates that leaders typically follow a cyclical pattern that includes tolerating the problem, trying to remediate the teacher's underperformance, or inducing the teacher to resign or to retire early. If the teacher does not improve or resign, then the principal recommends dismissal. The response of the leader sets the tone within the building.

Responses to Working with Underperforming Teachers

Underperforming teachers present challenges and opportunities for the school leadership. An underperforming teacher is one who has the potential to be effective but has some issues that are getting in the way. Regardless of the issue and the severity, a school leader must address the situation. The longer the teacher continues to perform poorly, the greater the negative impact will be on students. By being actively involved in the daily operations, the school leader has the ability to identify underperformance and respond proactively.

Severity of the Issues

Response to underperformance should match the severity of the issues. There is no need to put out a match with a bucket of water. The leader needs to assess the issue's severity. A teacher whose classroom is out of control is much different from a teacher who is struggling with transitions from one activity to another, probably even if five or so minutes are lost as a result. In all instances, formal and informal conversations should be part of the process of working with an underperforming teacher. It would hardly be the case that a plan of improvement would be the first course of action for a teacher having problems with transitions unless there were other related issues—for instance, students were off task and the teacher could not get them back on track for an inordinate amount of time. Regardless of the situation, teachers need and want support, they want to be encouraged as they take corrective action, and they want to feel as if their leader has confidence in their ability to improve.

Formal and Informal Approaches to Working with Underperforming Teachers

Informal approaches are locally developed and not necessarily covered by system, state, or federal policies. Informal approaches are typically not documented and do not become a part of the teacher's official file. Informal approaches could include, for example,

- participation in a book study with a group of teachers who are having similar difficulties;
- conversations with a coach, a peer, or even the leader as long as there is no formal record;
- pairing up with a peer coach; and
- observation of teachers who have strong skill sets in the area in which the teacher is having difficulty (e.g., perhaps a teacher in a different school within the system would be willing to host a struggling teacher for a day).

The astute leader scans the environment for opportunities for support, starting with informal approaches that are adjusted based on severity and progress toward goals.

Formal approaches are more official and may include some of the same approaches used informally, such as coaching and mentoring. However, the tenor of formal approaches changes with the dynamic of support because

- documentation is generated that details specific areas of concern;
- interventions are spelled out in detail in a plan of improvement (see Chapter 6) that becomes part of the underperforming teacher's file; and
- personnel recommendations could be the final step of the approach.

The Teacher's Response to Being Identified as an Underperformer

A teacher's response to being deemed underperforming will bring a variety of reactions. These reactions will be tempered by the approach of the principal, the relationship between the teacher and the principal, the number of years of experience for the teacher, and a host of other variables that are present at the school site (e.g., is the school a well-functioning one or a school put on notice for student low performance?). Response will also be predicated on the ways in which formative and summative aspects of teacher evaluation are carried out in the school: Are all teachers engaged in the same processes and procedures? Is the evaluator new to the position?

It is safe to assume (really, it is) that a teacher who is deemed underperforming will react negatively; however, there is hope that with the right types of supports, underperforming teachers can turn things around by taking the steps in the journey to improve performance in the classroom. The response of an underperforming teacher depends on the severity of the situation, how long the underperforming behaviors in the classroom have been present, and other issues that are specific to the context of the school.

Being evaluated is stressful in all professions. Reactions can run the gamut from acknowledging there is a problem to denial that there are issues that prevent teacher and student success. Consider the teacher whose performance is merely satisfactory in the area of using transitions between activities. That teacher is really not underperforming in the overall scheme of things; however, instructional time is being wasted, and some students do take advantage of the seemingly chaotic minute or two between each activity. If the teacher has three transitions in an hour and there is a 2-minute gap between the activities, students would lose 6 minutes of instruction per day, 30 minutes per week, 120 minutes per month, 1,080 minutes per year, or 18 hours (an equivalent of 18 class periods) annually. Now, consider the teacher whose 1-hour class is disorganized such that instruction is fragmented to the extent that students get even less focused time.

Both teachers are not performing in the classroom but in very different ways. These examples illustrate why school leaders need to know their teachers and classroom learning environments and have a solid foundation for giving feedback and engaging in conversations that focus on student learning (see Chapter 5). This lofty set of goals, however, can get complicated by the range of responses: Disbelief, anger, denial, and relief are a few of the infinite responses.

Disbelief

Disbelief is "a feeling that you do not or cannot believe or accept that something is true or real" ("disbelief," n.d.). Often, people are not aware that there is an issue: They might have blinders on or be so close to the problem that they cannot recognize that there is a problem or, even if they do recognize that a problem exists, they do not know objectively how to address the issue.

Joseph Luft and Harry Ingham (1955) developed the Johari Window to describe personal knowledge and interactions in terms of four panes:

- *Open pane*: information that is known by the person and others; information is shared and public.

- *Hidden pane*: information that is known by the person but hidden from others as in a public persona.
- *Blind pane*: information that is factual but unknown by the person as it is a blind spot.
- *Unknown pane*: information that is not known to the person or to others—the unknown pane is a person's unconsciousness.

Figure 4.1 illustrates the Johari Window and how information can support the deepening of teachers' understandings about their efforts.

A teacher's response of disbelief might stem from a blind spot causing unawareness about an issue. As the principal, you can assist teachers in seeing blind spots related to instruction, assessment, and other arrangements in the classroom by

- engaging in conversations after classroom observations;
- enlisting the support of a peer coach to work with struggling teachers;
- arranging for the teacher to observe an accomplished teacher; and
- recording a classroom segment and viewing the segment with the teacher.

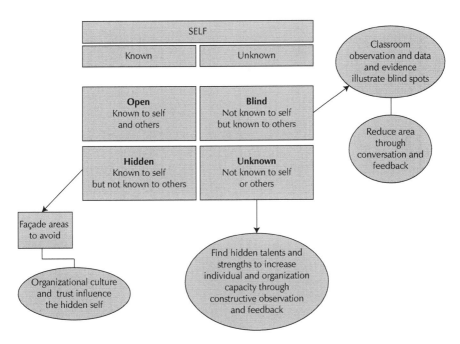

Figure 4.1   The Johari Window—Deepening Teacher Understanding

Denial

Denial is the evil cousin to disbelief. For the purposes of this book, *denial* is "a condition in which someone will not admit that something sad, painful, or the like is true or real" ("denial," n.d.). A person is in denial when he/she fails to acknowledge that there is an issue. As the leader, it falls to you to engage in conversations that are filled with objective, hard data to illustrate the area in need of improvement.

Anger

Anger is an emotional response. The teacher could become passive-aggressive (McEwan, 2005) in which the teacher raises his/her voice, uses inappropriate langue, threatens to call the union, or even leaves the discussion either figuratively or physically. Again, the severity of the reaction dictates the principal's response, which could include helping the angry teacher absorb and make rational sense of feedback.

Resistance

There is a three-part definition to *resistance* that includes "refusal to accept something new or different; effort made to stop or to fight against someone or something; [and] the ability to prevent something from having an effect" ("resistance," n.d.). If you are working with underperforming teachers, essentially you are asking teachers to make changes in one or more of their practices. McEwan (2005) and Eller and Eller (2010) reported that resistant teachers had difficulty accepting and adapting to change, more seasoned teachers were resistant to change, and curricular and instructional modifications were not in use because of their beliefs about the effort it would take to change (i.e., too much work). The severity of the issues would dictate the types of conversations and the levels of assistance (informal or formal).

Relief

A very different response would be *relief*, defined as "the removal" or "reduction of something that is painful or unpleasant" ("relief," n.d.). Looking at objective data collected across several sources of artifacts and evidence (e.g., classroom observation notes, lesson plans, and samples of student work), a teacher who is having issues could feel a sense of relief because help is on the way through specific feedback, suggestions about areas for improvement, and appropriate resources.

The responses a teacher offers to underperformance is a wild card and points to the types of conversations that a leader and teacher could have. In Chapter 5, conversations about teaching and learning focused on underperforming teachers are examined in detail.

References

Bauerlein, M. (2013, May 17). Sunday Points [Editorial]. Among young workers, a growing sense of entitlement. *The Dallas Morning News*. Retrieved from http://www.dallasnews.com/opinion/sunday-commentary/20130517-mark-bauerlein-among-young-workers-a-growing-sense-of-entitlement.ece

Bolch, M. (2015). Have a few bad apples? *Administrative Magazine*. Retrieved from http://www.scholastic.com/browse/article.jsp?id=11390

Bridges, E. M. (1992). *The incompetent teacher: Managerial responses*. London: Falmer Press.

Campbell, W. K., Bonacci, A. M., Shelton, J., Exline, J., & Bushman, B. J. (2004). Psychological entitlement: Interpersonal consequences and validation of a self-report measure. *Journal of Personality Assessment, 83*(1), 29–45. doi: 10.1207/s15327752jpa8301_04

Coggshall, J. G., Behrstock-Sherratt, E., & Drill, K. (2011). *Workplaces that support high-performing teaching and learning: Insights from Generation Y teachers*. Washington, D.C.: American Federation of Teachers & American Institutes for Research. Retrieved from http://www.air.org/resource/workplaces-support-high-performing-teaching-and-learning-insights-generation-y-teachers

Darling-Hammond, L. (2012). *Creating a comprehensive system for evaluating and supporting effective teaching*. Stanford: Stanford Center for Opportunity Policy in Education. Retrieved from https://edpolicy.stanford.edu

Denial. (n.d.). In *Merriam-Webster online*. Retrieved from http://www.merriam-webster.com/dictionary/denial

Disbelief. (n.d.) In *Merriam-Webster online*. Retrieved from http://www.merriam-webster.com/dictionary/disbelief

Eller, J. F., & Eller, S. (2010). *Working with and evaluating difficult school employees*. Thousand Oaks, CA: Corwin.

Entitlement generation. (n.d.). *Dictionary.com's 21st century lexicon*. Retrieved July 12, 2015, from Dictionary.com website: http://dictionary.reference.com/browse/entitlement generation

Foster, K. R. (2013). *Generation, discourse, and social change*. New York: Routledge.

Fuhr, D. (1990). Supervising the marginal teacher: Here's how. *National Association of Elementary Teachers, 9*(2), 1–4. Retrieved from http://www.eric.ed.gov:80/PDFS/ED324825.pdf

Goldring, R., Taie, S., & Riddles, M. (2014). *Teacher attrition and mobility: Results from the 2012–13 teacher follow-up survey* (NCES 2014-077). U.S. Department of Education. Washington, D.C.: National Center for Education Statistics. Retrieved from http://nces.ed.gov/pubsearch

Hughes, J. (Producer and Director). (1986). *Ferris Bueller's day off* [Motion picture]. United States: Paramount Pictures.

Ingersoll, R., & Merrill, L. (2010). Who's teaching our children? *Educational Leadership, 67*(8), 14–20. Retrieved from http://www.ascd.org/publications/educational-leadership/may10/vol67/num08/Who%27s-Teaching-Our-Children%C2%A2.aspx

Ingersoll, R., Merrill, L., & Stuckey, D. (2014). *Seven trends: The transformation of the teaching force. CPRE Report (#RR-80)*. Philadelphia: Consortium for Policy Research in Education, University of Pennsylvania.

Luft, J., & Ingham, H. (1955). *The Johari Window: A graphic model for interpersonal relations*. University of California Western Training Lab.

McEwan, E. (2005). *How to deal with teachers who are angry, troubled, exhausted, or just plain confused*. Thousand Oaks, CA: Corwin.

Nolan, J., Jr., & Hoover, L. A. (2011). *Teacher supervision and evaluation: Theory into practice* (3rd ed.). Hoboken, NJ: John Wiley & Sons.

Performance Management Consulting, LLC. (2013). *Entitlement mentality. Earning employee excellence*. Author. Retrieved from http://p-m-consult.com/Entitle.html

Relief. (n.d.) In *Merriam-Webster's online*. Retrieved from http://www.merriam-webster.com/dictionary/relief

Resistance. (n.d.) In *Merriam-Webster's online*. Retrieved from http://www.merriam-webster.com/dictionary/resistance

Rourke, K. S. (2011). You owe me: Examining a generation of entitlement. *Student Pulse, 3*(1). Retrieved from http://www.studentpulse.com/articles/362/you-owe-me-examining-a-generation-of-entitlement

Russo, A. (Producer), & Hiller, A. (Director). (1984). *Teachers* [Motion picture]. United States: MGM/UA Entertainment Company.

Smith, R. E. (2008). *Human resources administration: A school-based perspective* (4th ed.). New York: Routledge.

Stiggins, R. (2014). *Defensible teacher evaluation: Student growth through classroom assessment*. Thousand Oaks, CA: Corwin.

Twenge, J. M., Campbell, S. M., Hoffman, B. J., & Lance, C. E. (2010) Generational differences in work values: Leisure and extrinsic values increasing, social and intrinsic values decreasing. *Journal of Management, 36*(5), 1117–1142. doi: 10.1177/0149206309352246

Walvoord, B., & Anderson, V. J. (1998). *Effective grading: A tool for learning and assessment*. San Francisco: Jossey-Bass.

Zepeda, S. J. (2011). *Duties and responsibilities: Teacher evaluation system for the Clarke County School District*. Athens, GA: Clarke County School District.

Zepeda, S. J. (2013). *The principal as instructional leader: A practical handbook* (3rd ed.). New York: Routledge.

Zitek, E. M., Jordan, A. H., Monin, B., & Leach, F. R. (2010). Victim entitlement to behave selfishly. *Journal of Personality and Social Psychology, 98*(2), 245–255. doi: 10.1037/a0017168

5 | Conversations Needed to Work with Underperforming Teachers

In this chapter ...

- Approaching Opportunities and Challenges Inherent in Conversations
- Unpacking Types of Conversations
- Creating the Conditions for Conversations
- Getting Ready for Difficult Conversations
- Key Communication Strategies for Working with Underperforming Teachers

Conversations are the cornerstone of working with and supporting teachers. Many factors are associated with having productive conversations with teachers who are underperforming. Some factors that impact conversations might entail the experience level of the leader, the relationship among administrators and the union (e.g., collective bargaining), and the relationship between the principal and the teacher. There has been a press for the value of conversations as a leadership tool (Groysberg & Slind, 2012; Jackson, 2013), the importance of conversations that are courageous (Hayashi, 2011), fierce (Scott, 2004, 2009), crucial (Patterson, Grenny, McMillan, & Switzler, 2012), change oriented (Hayashi, 2011), and just plain difficult to have (Abrams, 2009; Eller & Eller, 2010; Shields, 2009).

Approaching Opportunities and Challenges Inherent in Conversations

Engaging in conversations about teacher performance necessitates that leaders step out of their comfort zones to be able to take the necessary actions and risks to ensure that all children are being taught by teachers who press learning while holding that children are the reason they teach. Effective leaders prioritize to find the uninterrupted time to focus on conversations about teaching and learning. Conversations that focus on teaching and learning are not automatic ones that occur from the hip; however, spontaneous conversations occur every day in the hallways, the copy room, or any other place in which teachers and leaders spend their time before, during, and after school. Leaders become opportunistic by finding the time and space to engage in conversations with all teachers.

Opportunities and Challenges

By engaging in conversations based on teaching and the artifacts that point to strengths and weaknesses, leaders are actively involving teachers in examining their own practices. This type of active involvement can reap many rewards—namely, applying strengths to help the teacher move to the next level and, conversely, helping teachers pinpoint areas that need support. Refer back to Chapter 4 and re-examine the Johari Window. Recall that there are four panes—open, hidden, blind, and unknown—as illustrated in Figure 4.1. With underperforming teachers, it is more than likely that conversations about practice would have the leader pinpointing areas within the hidden, blind, or unknown panes. Let's take the case of Janet Smith:

> Janet Smith, a 13-year veteran mathematics teacher, has had issues since the implementation of the Common Core State Standards. Her instructional performance has waned, and there have been some content-related issues. There are class periods during which it appears that her students are seeking clarification that she cannot give to them. During grade-level meetings, Janet chimes in that the "kids are just plain lazy and do not want to get with the program."

The quadrants of the Johari Window can become "larger" or "smaller" as Janet becomes aware of blind spots magnified through stable data from two sources: classroom observations and performance observations at grade-level meetings. Specific data from classroom observations and first-hand observations of Janet interacting with her colleagues at grade-level meetings helps the leader frame the conversation. It appears that Janet is struggling with adapting her instruction to the new standards, and she is blaming children as a possible way to rationalize her own performance.

As the leader, it falls to you to have a conversation that addresses these issues in a way that opens understanding, to support Janet in identifying professional learning opportunities (e.g., observing another grade-level teacher), and to target an actionable plan to improve Janet's instructional issues. Conversations are complex, however. The part of the conversation about Janet's beliefs about students might be much more difficult than the parts about her issues with adapting to the new standards, because her statements encompass the belief or attitude that students are lazy. As the leader, you must maintain a delicate balance because attitudes can adversely impact performance. Janet's comments to her colleagues could potentially put a pall on the ways in which team members interact, negatively affecting the workflow of the team. Depending on the composition of the team, the context of the school, and the school's culture, Janet could be fueling negativity that, if not addressed, could lead to larger issues in the school such as dips in teacher morale or worse, perpetuating the belief that "kids are just plain lazy."

Approaching underperformance is a challenge because people do not like to engage in the risky behavior known as *confrontation*. Conversations that confront and challenge are awkward because we have been brought up to be polite, to go along to get along, and not to offend anyone. Later, politeness theory and saving face are examined in the context of conversations, giving feedback, and offering constructive criticism in the context of teaching and learning. The issues of underperforming teachers will not magically go away. Many of these problems are patterns that have been reinforced for years, and many of these behaviors and attitudes are ingrained in the way people think. These bad habits have now become glaring weaknesses in specified areas. Think of the consequences if you do not engage in the conversations related to underperformance:

1   Those who are performing well will walk away with the message that it's okay to slip and slide; leaders are oblivious or they do not care or they avoid issues.

2   Issues that can be resolved never make it to the conversation for problem-solving, strategy development, or resources that could help a teacher to strengthen skills and practices or work on attitude issues.

3   The issues begin to escalate or carry over into other closely related areas. For example, an issue with course content could negatively affect instruction, assessment, or classroom management.

The conversations promoted in this book are informed by data, among which are classroom observations, student work exemplars, results from student and parent surveys, and student progress as measured on internal and external tests. The conversations also promote bringing people to the table to examine strengths (what's working) and areas of concern (what's not working, why, and how to identify solutions). To be more effective, school-based leaders need to unpack the types of conversations that will engage teachers in learning.

Unpacking Types of Conversations

Informally, we communicate every day across a variety of mediums including blogs, Twitter, Facebook, and Pinterest, and with chats with colleagues and leaders between class periods, in the hallways, or in the parking lot. More formally, leaders engage in conversations during formal post-observation conferences, summative evaluation meetings, goal-setting sessions, and the like. Communication with teachers is ether formal or informal. Regardless of the type, conversations should be the forum where teachers and leaders can speak honestly and where facts, evidence, and other rational means carry forward the discussion. Conversation must not devolve into blaming and shaming sessions. Conversations are more than two people just talking to one another.

With underperforming teachers, conversations shift by focusing on very specific evidence or actions that capture performance deficiencies and conclude, more than likely, with very specific details on what must be done to improve, how improvement must be enacted, and guidelines and possible resources that could help the underperforming teacher to meet performance expectations related to teaching, classroom management, assessment, behaviors at grade-level meetings, or whichever duties and responsibilities are at issue. Chapter 6 details plans of improvement that include intensive and formal forms of communication both orally and in writing.

Conversation Types

Formal and Informal Conversations

Formal conversations are pre-planned conversations such as a post-observation conference or a meeting to discuss student achievement, and these types of conversation occur with all teachers. Formal conversations necessitate pre-planning by the leader. Without preparation, credibility diminishes. Later in the chapter, preparation for formal conversations is examined.

Informal conversations are the ones that occur in the moment and center on a variety of topics. Informal conversations also provide a forum completely devoid of value judgment so teachers are free to share successes and difficulties with their practices. Effective leaders enlarge the conversation by making one informal conversation with a teacher segue to the next. In other words, conversations with individuals or groups of teachers are continuous and follow a thread throughout the year. To enlarge the discussion, leaders need always to be looking for ways to incorporate teaching, learning, and students as the core of the conversation. The messages in these conversations must offer a consistent message, focusing more on the instructional program and what is occurring in classrooms, grade-level meetings, and the like.

Crucial and Fierce Conversations

Patterson et al. (2012) define a crucial conversation as "a discussion between two or more people where (1) stakes are high, (2) opinions vary, and (3) emotions run strong" (p. 3). The stakes are indeed very high for all teachers, especially those who are struggling with any aspect of their performance that has a negative impact on student learning. According to Scott (2004), "*a fierce conversation is one in which we come out from behind ourselves into the conversation and make it real*" (p. 7, emphasis in the original).

Difficult Conversations

Nobody likes to hear about or discuss their weaknesses. The difficulty of the conversation will be related to the issues that a teacher is experiencing.

Conversations with an underperforming teacher at the beginning of the year might look very different as the year progresses. The difficulty of the conversation is dependent on a host of factors, including, for example, the severity of the issues. Difficult conversations with underperforming teachers must, regardless of content, provide a safe place where

- high-quality support is offered as a continuous process;
- time and efforts are focused on developing strategies for teachers to improve their practices;
- conversations are purposeful, with feedback offered in a way that teachers can save face regardless of the circumstances; and
- conversations include a variety of effective questioning and feedback.

At the end of every conversation, an ongoing and open invitation for the next conversation is presented.

Using Questions Wisely

Regardless of the type of conversation, questions play an integral part. Generally speaking, there are four types of questions—probing, open, closed, and extended recall—which are outlined in Table 5.1.

To ensure that conversations are productive, there are a few conditions that can support the exchange of ideas and that can help the principal bring good intentions to working with underperforming teachers.

Creating the Conditions for Conversations

The quality of conversations in any school building is dependent on the relationships that school leaders have with teachers, the relationships that teachers have with one another, and the school's culture, including norms, values, and beliefs that teachers hold for themselves and students. The leader must be adept with building relationships with teachers, and Scott (2004) reminds us that the conversation in many ways "is the relationship" (p. 5). Conversations help teachers to (1) build professional practices as they continue to improve on instructional strategies that worked; (2) reflect on teaching practices; and (3) share professional knowledge and expertise.

Table 5.1 Types of Questions

Type of question	Intent(s)	Question examples
Probing	Promote deeper thought	• Would you tell me more about …? • Why do you suppose X occurred during the lesson?
Open	Promote going beyond short one- or two-worded responses to encouraging conversations; to relate more details about specific practices; or to help fill in the blanks with information that might not be readily known or understood.	• Can you explain the benefit your students have derived from using more open-ended questions? • What lessons have you learned from changing your instructional approach based on student data?
Closed	Promotes simple yes or no or other short, factual responses that place the control of the conversation with the person asking the questions; closed questions do not promote two-way, interactive conversations.	• Did you prepare your lesson plan according to the district framework? • Will you follow up with a quiz tomorrow?
Extended recall	Promotes going into detail about a specific incident to start attaching more meanings through reflection and questioning.	• Think back to [some aspect of the lesson or the class] and tell me about it. • Tell me more about [some aspect of the class, student response, an instructional method, etc.].

Adapted from Zepeda (2015)

School Culture

Leaders recognize the importance of creating a growth-oriented culture that encourages formal and informal conversations and feedback on practice. Gruenert and Whitaker (2015) share that the school's culture, including vestiges to past practices, can render conversations as "frequent and voluntary or rare and mandated; merely congenial or genuinely productive" (p. 73). A culture marked as collaborative would, according to Nelson (2013), be able to withstand and embrace tough questions. As a leader, reflect on the following three questions offered by Nelson (2013):

1 What does a "hard conversation" about teaching and learning look like?
2 When have we had those conversations in our school and when have we avoided them?

3 When has a conversation with colleagues had an impact on your practice?

(para. 9)

These questions could be used in several ways: (1) as a way for the leader and the leadership team to commit to engaging in difficult conversations as a priority for the year, (2) as a way to engage the entire school in preparing to make conversations a priority, and (3) as a tool for leaders and teachers to reflect on the importance of questions as a way to spark conversations about teaching, learning, and the improvement of practice.

School Climate

The National School Climate Council (2007) indicates that

School climate refers to the quality and character of school life. School climate is based on patterns of students', parents', and school personnel's experience of school life and reflects norms, goals, values, interpersonal relationships, teaching and learning practices, and organizational structures.

(p. 5)

The school climate dictates whether teachers collaborate with one another and whether interactions are collegial and inviting. An environment of open discussion fosters adult learning.

Norms

Norms are unwritten rules of behavior that serve as a guide to the way people interact with one another (Chance, 2009). Norms are important to conversations and the ways in which leaders interact with teachers. Baseline norms to encourage conversations would include being respectful by listening intently to what the other person has to say; answering questions as they arise or following up with an answer as soon as possible; avoiding cutting off a teacher who is in mid-stream of a thought or a sentence; and ensuring that teachers feel valued—even if a teacher is struggling, entering a plan of improvement, or being told that non-renewal is imminent.

Trust, Respect, and Civility

Conversations are enhanced when there is trust. Shields (2004) reminds us that

> Dialogue and relationships are not elements that can be selected and discarded at will; rather, they are ways of life—recognitions of the fundamental differences among human beings and of the need to enter into contact, into relational dialogue and sense making ... with one another.
>
> (p. 116)

Without trust, relationships flounder. Trust and respect build a strong foundation for the work and efforts of teachers. Effective school leaders develop relational trust that rests on a foundation of respect, personal regard, and integrity. Relational trust flourishes when all can contribute, learn, and be part of the conversations about teaching and student learning.

Presence

Teachers need and want to have access to school leaders throughout the day, and teachers want their school leaders to have a visible presence (Zepeda & Ponticell, 1998). School leaders feel the tug-of-war when they are out of the building attending meetings at the central office or fulfilling other duties and responsibilities that take them away from the schoolhouse. However, school leaders have to do a better job at being "out and about" in the hallways and in classrooms most especially.

Getting Ready for Difficult Conversations

Entering a difficult conversation without the proper preparation is akin to leaving for a long-distance road trip without fuel in your car, a road map, and a clear destination in mind. The amount of preparation for a difficult conversation with an underperforming teacher depends on the seriousness of the situation and when in the school year it is occurring—the beginning of the year, at the midpoint, or a week before non-renewal notices will be issued. Many other factors also influence preparation and depend on the unique situation that precipitates the conversation, the context of the issues, and the overall history of the teacher (e.g., whether the teacher repeatedly underperforms in and out of the classroom). Eller and Eller (2012, p. 30) make it very clear that "the most successful difficult conversations are well planned, clear, and let the employee know that the principal means business" (p. 30).

Preparing for the Conversation

The following cues are offered to assist school leaders in preparing for a formal conversation with a teacher. The reader is encouraged to adapt these cues to fit the context and the circumstances surrounding the discussion.

Intent

Start by asking three questions:

1   Why is the conversation being initiated?
2   What is the motivation for engaging in the conversation?
3   Most important, what are the goals for the conversation?

The leader needs to know what understanding needs to be reached by the end of the conversation. To keep focused, bring cue cards with the goals elaborated in 1, 2, 3, fashion as illustrated here:

Teacher:_____   Date: _____   Time:_____

Meeting Location:_____ Present:_____

Meeting Goals
Goal 1:
Goal 2:
Goal 3:

Issues

With the goals in mind, identify the issues that need to be addressed during the conversation, or the "why we are gathered" elaboration of the issues. Be very specific about the issues as they relate to performance in or out of the classroom. Frame the issues broadly and then be able to fill in with details.

Issues
Issue 1:
Issue 2:
Issue 3:

Evidence and Examples

Just as the goals of the conversation and the issues need to be clearly stated, the evidence and the examples that point to underperformance need to be elaborated orally and with as many documents as possible. In many ways, the documentation and evidence will be invaluable if the underperformance is not rectified in a timely manner. The next logical step would be to move toward a formal plan of improvement (see Chapter 6).

Issues	Detail Highlights	Artifacts and Evidence
Issue 1:		
Issue 2:		
Issue 3:		

Determining What's at Stake

For every issue, there is an impact that leads to identifying what is at stake for students, teachers, or even the school. These questions can help you frame the deleterious impact of underperformance:

1 Are students being negatively impacted by underperformance in the classroom?

2 Is the quality of team meetings being compromised because a teacher is difficult in that he or she is not adding to the value of what needs to get accomplished to support learning for all students at a particular grade level or subject area?

3 Is a teacher's habit of arriving late, leaving early, or calling in sick depleting other human resources?

4 Is the underperformance causing a disruption to student learning?

Let the artifacts and evidence propel this part of the conversation.

Issues	Detail Highlights	Artifacts and Evidence	Impact
Issue 1:			
Issue 2:			
Issue 3:			

Establishing Expectations and Timelines

For every issue, the leader needs to establish an expectation for improvement and a timeline. The teacher may also need resources, so have some ideas about what resources are readily available in the school or perhaps even in the system. Explain the types of follow-up that will be provided.

Issues	Expected Changes in Performance and Timeline
Issue 1:	
Issue 2:	
Issue 3:	

Helpful Suggestions to Guide a Difficult Conversation

The following suggestions are offered to further assist with a difficult conversation.

Time

Determine how much time you think it will take to review the contents of the conversation. Typically, the school leader would meet with a teacher before, during, or after school. Check local policies and union agreements to determine whether meeting at a particular time during the day would be supported by the union and the central office. Attention span, perhaps anger, would necessitate meeting more than one time.

Meeting Location

Many leaders like to have difficult conversations in the teacher's classroom or an office. The location should be private as the conversation and its contents are confidential. The meeting space should be quiet and free from interruptions.

Suspension of Judgment

Although honesty is always the best policy, refrain from making value judgments about teachers and their struggles.

Key Communication Strategies for Working with Underperforming Teachers

Characteristics of Feedback

Feedback—some people ask for it while others do not want it, and perhaps Frase's (1992) findings helps us to understand why: "[F]eedback has too often been inaccurate, shallow and at times mean spirited, rather than helpful and uplifting" (p. 179). Ovando (2005) shares, "Feedback refers to relevant

Table 5.2 Characteristics of Effective Feedback

Effective feedback ...
• is constructive (Zepeda, 2015);
• is timely and specific because "Teachers should not be left in the dark about what the principal thinks" (Marshall, 2005, p. 728);
• is relevant to individual teachers' needs (Wilkins-Canter, 1997);
• promotes teacher growth and learning (Feeney, 2007); and
• is more readily accepted if the provider has credibility (Roberts, 2003; Zepeda, 2013).

information provided to those engaged in the teaching and learning process regarding their performance so that they may introduce modifications, correct errors or engage in professional development that will lead to enhanced teaching and learning" (p. 173). The major goal is for feedback to improve the effectiveness of teaching and to promote professional growth (Feeney, 2007). To satisfy this goal, feedback should be

1   grounded in practice and collected in a non-judgmental and descriptive manner to capture actual practices;
2   linked to the characteristics of effective teaching; and
3   a beginning point to promote reflection, problem-posing, and so forth as a means to foster improvements in teaching supported by evidence of student learning.

Crane (2002) tells us that "effective feedback allows the receiver to maintain a sense of dignity, self-respect, and control over his or her choices or how to respond to the feedback" (p. 75). To achieve these goals, then, feedback must have certain characteristics, as outlined in Table 5.2.

The Language of Feedback

There is a language to feedback that either motivates or demotivates teachers (Zepeda, 2015). In the coaching literature, Carr, Herman, and Harris (2005) present three broad categories to classify feedback expressions: mirror, collaborative, and expert. Each one of the categories represents a different intent for the conversation. For example, in the process of *mirroring*, the coach is holding a mirror up to reflect practice as it occurs in the situation. Gall and Acheson's (2010) analogy is that the supervisor acts as a mirror to a teacher's

Table 5.3 Coaching Feedback

Broad category	Intents	Examples
Mirror	The coach tells a teacher what he or she did or said to provide the teacher with feedback, which encourages reflective learning.	• I noticed you tried... • I saw you do...
Collaborative	The coach and teacher share collectively their thoughts as a way to foster conversations, to inquire about practice, and to generate ideas together.	• Let's try together... • How do you think it went? • What would this new practice look like in your classroom tomorrow?
Expert	The coach tells (subtly directs) teachers what they need to do in order to grasp new understandings or changes in practice.	• You could do... • Try doing this... • This is the way... • If you want [this] result, then try [this].

practice by taking heavily scripted notes during a classroom observation that can then be used to reconstruct the events of the classroom (Zepeda, 2012, 2013). During the process of *collaborating*, the coach and the teacher collectively engage in sharing thoughts and ideas as a way to generate new ideas or to refine existing ideas and practices. In the *expert* approach, the coach "tells" the teacher specific information by suggesting new approaches. Table 5.3 provides some feedback examples of the broad categories of coaching as envisioned by Carr et al. (2005).

The Emotional Side of Feedback

Have you ever wondered why some people get defensive about feedback? Was the defensiveness caused by the choice of words, the body language of the person giving the feedback, the timing of the feedback, or some other unknown variable? If a teacher does not want feedback, then chances are the principal will be met with resistance or resentment. The feedback may be viewed as a power play. A teacher who is receiving feedback that focuses on weaknesses will be less than satisfied with the situation. Emotions can run the gamut. A leader cannot expect to have a productive meeting and conversation with a disappointed, defensive, or angry teacher who is receiving less than stellar feedback.

When dealing with an underperforming teacher, regardless of the severity, honest feedback presented professionally is what is needed. Here are a few suggestions to support efforts of working with a teacher who may be resentful or resistant to feedback.

1   Remain neutral and stick to only the facts.
2   Refrain from showing impatience, talking over the teacher, and so on.
3   Acknowledge the resentment but press forward with the feedback surrounding the facts.
4   Cut the meeting length and reschedule another meeting to continue the feedback session. Depending on the severity of circumstances, feedback might be more easily digested in shorter blocks of time.
5   Remember, the feedback is not about the person; the feedback is about performance issues.
6   Try to infuse positive feedback with the negative. It is highly doubtful that a classroom observation would be so off the trail that there were no high points in what was observed.
7   Remain constructive in your approach; the intent of feedback is to help people to grow and develop.
8   Develop follow-up plans to support the teacher after meeting. Feedback can be offered but not necessarily acted on; a follow-up strategy helps keep the leader on track to ensure that progress toward improvement is occurring.

The closer a principal gets to making decisions about the likelihood that a teacher will not be returning (e.g., non-renewal), it is probably wise to have another administrator attend the meeting. As the saying goes, in desperate times, people do desperate things, and a witness might be beneficial for both the leader and the teacher.

Feedback Versus Criticism

In the broadest sense, *criticism* is defined as

1   the act of passing judgment as to the merits of anything.
2   the act of passing severe judgment; censure; faultfinding.

("criticism," n.d.)

The term *criticism* evokes an image of harshness; however, criticism is a form of feedback or critique, as in what film or literary critics do on the opening night of a film or play. When providing criticism, the leader needs to adhere to the same principles that govern feedback, such as being positive and objective, specific, and relevant to the situation. The major intent should be to foster growth and development.

Saving Face

Saving face is an important concept to keep in the forefront when working with all teachers, especially those who are underperforming. People have basic needs including feeling valued, being affirmed for their efforts, and being able to save face when their performance is less than stellar. As a golden rule, a teacher who is not experiencing success in the classroom needs direct assistance, but this assistance must be given in such a way that the teacher (1) fully recognizes there are issues, (2) understands that improvements must be made in a timely manner, and (3) can walk away from the conversation with his or her dignity intact. An underperforming teacher can save face knowing that you, the principal, are willing to help and that he or she is able to do what needs to be done to improve.

When dignity is stripped, there is little hope for the teacher and for the principal—little hope of motivating the teacher toward the path of improvement or of maintaining trust and a relationship with the teacher. We don't want teachers counting the months until the plan of improvement expires or non-renewal is impending. We want teachers who can reach inside of themselves to rectify the issues and who are supported along the way. However, we need principals who communicate in a tactful but direct way with teachers who are underperforming. *Sugar-coating* (or *hedging*) is the use of evasive language to communicate a serious issue. Sugar-coating takes the form not only of the words used but also the facial expressions, tone of voice, and other signals displayed. Choose words and behaviors wisely!

Face Saving: A Two-Way Street

During a conversation, there is two-way communication directed by words, eye contact, body language, and perceived attentiveness to the message each party wants to impart. Anytime two people engage in conversation, potentially face-saving communication transpires. Confronting and working with underperformance occurs during conversations with teachers. Often, conversations lack clarity. Part of the reason for this vagueness is because of the fear of hurting the other person's feelings or the fear of repercussions: What will that person think of me? What will that person share with his or her colleagues in the faculty lounge? What will be communicated to the union that could potentially lead to a grievance?

Face-Saving Conversations and Politeness Theory

From the field of linguistics emerges politeness theory, which boils down to the words, phrases, and other verbal utterances we choose to use and the ways the person on the other end interprets or reacts to what we are saying. Yule (1996) tells us that politeness is "showing awareness of another person's face", that face-threatening acts occur when there is "a threat to another person's self-image," and that face-saving acts occur when you are "saying something that lessens the possible threat to another's face" (p. 134). There are several instances when a leader will engage in conversations with an underperforming teacher—a post-observation conference, a meeting to review the plan of improvement, informal check-ins to get a sense of progress from a teacher, and so on.

Rowland (1999) reports that Brown and Levinson (1987) examined conversations and found "speakers avoid threats to the 'face' of those they address by various forms of indirectness, vagueness, and so on, and thereby 'implicate' (hint at) their meanings rather than assert them directly" (p. 86). Positive face, according to Rowland, is "a desire to be appreciated and valued by others; desire for approval" (p. 86). No one wants to deliver bad news but the principal must rise to the occasion in such a way that both the leader and the teacher can save face. Rowland (1995, 1999) offers several language strategies used to hide as people communicate to save face while delivering a message. One such strategy is hedging, which Tang (2013) indicates is a negative politeness strategy used to avoid disagreement. Let's take, for example, a teacher whose classroom is chaotic and in which students are out of control. During the post-observation conference, the principal shares with the teacher this advice: "Maybe you should take a class period and refresh student understanding of classroom behavior standards." The use of "maybe" is a hedging technique that serves to soften the blow that the teacher needs to regain control.

Conversations continue individually and collectively within a school, with the leader encouraging such exchanges. Conversations will change over time, especially between a principal and an underperforming teacher. Conversations with underperforming teachers intensify with the movement to a plan of improvement, examined next in Chapter 6.

References

Abrams, J. (2009). *Having hard conversations*. Thousand Oaks, CA: Corwin.

Carr, J., Herman, N., & Harris, D. (2005). *Creating dynamic schools through mentoring, coaching, and collaboration*. Alexandria, VA: Association for Supervision and Curriculum Development.

Chance, P. L. (2009). *Introduction to educational leadership and organizational behavior: Theory into practice* (2nd ed.). New York: Routledge.

Crane, T. G. (2002). *The heart of coaching: Using transformational coaching to create a high-performance coaching culture* (2nd ed.). San Diego: FTA Press.

Criticism. (n.d.). In *dictionary.com*. Retrieved from http://dictionary.reference.com/browse/criticism

Eller, J. F., & Eller, S. A. (2010). *Working with and evaluating difficult school employees*. Thousand Oaks, CA: Corwin.

Eller, J. F., & Eller, S. A. (2012). Working productively with difficult and resistant staff. *Principal,* September/October, 28–31. Retrieved from http://www.naesp.org/sites/default/files/Eller_SO12.pdf

Feeney, E. J. (2007). Quality feedback: The essential ingredient for teacher success. *The Clearing House, 80*(4), 191–197. Retrieved from http://eric.ed.gov/?id=EJ771291

Frase, L. E. (1992). Constructive feedback on teaching is missing. *Education, 113*(2), 176–181. Retrieved from http://www.projectinnovation.biz/education

Gall, M. D., & Acheson, K. A. (2010). *Clinical supervision and teacher development* (6th ed.). Hoboken, NJ: John Wiley & Sons.

Groysberg, B., & Slind, M. (2012). *Talk, Inc.* Boston: Harvard Business School Publishing.

Gruenert, S., & Whitaker, T. (2015). *School culture rewired: How to define, assess, and transform it*. Alexandria, VA: Association of Supervision and Curriculum Development.

Hayashi, S. K. (2011). *Conversations for change: 12 ways to say it right when it matters most*. New York: McGraw-Hill.

Jackson, J. (2013). *Get a backbone, principal: 5 conversations every school leader must have right now!* Denver: Outskirts Press.

Marshall, K. (2005). It's time to rethink teacher supervision and evaluation. *Phi Delta Kappan, 86*(10), 727–730. Retrieved from http://pdkintl.org/publications/kappan

National School Climate Council. (2007). *The school climate challenge: Narrowing the gap between school climate research and school climate policy, practice guidelines and teacher education policy*. New York: National School Climate Center. Retrieved from: http://nscc.csee.net

Nelson, C. (2013). *Building a collaborative culture that values deep conversations.* Westerville, OH: Association for Middle Level Education. Retrieved from http://www.amle.org/BrowsebyTopic/WhatsNew/WNDet.aspx?ArtMID=888&ArticleID=345

Ovando, M. N. (2005). Building instructional leaders' capacity to deliver constructive feedback to teachers. *Journal of Personnel Evaluation in Education, 18*(3), 171–183. doi: 10.1007/s11092-006-9018-z

Patterson, K., Grenny, J, McMillan, R., & Switzler, A. (2012). *Crucial conversations: Tools for talking when stakes are high* (2nd ed.). New York: McGraw-Hill.

Roberts, G. E. (2003). Employee performance appraisal system participation: A technique that works. *Public Personnel Management, 30*(1), 333–342. Retrieved from http://ppm.sagepub.com

Rowland, T. (1995). Hedges in mathematics talk: Linguistic pointers to uncertainty. *Educational Studies in Mathematics, 29*(4), 327–353. doi: 10.1007/BF01273910

Rowland, T. (1999). *The pragmatics of mathematics education: Vagueness in mathematical discourse.* London: Falmer Press.

Scott, S. (2004). *Fierce conversations: Achieving success at work and in life one conversation at a time.* New York: Berkley Books.

Shields, C. M. (2004). Dialogic leadership for social justice: Overcoming pathologies of silence. *Educational Administrator Quarterly 40*(1), 109–132. doi:10.1177/0013161X03258963

Shields, C. M. (2009). Introduction. In *Courageous leadership for transforming schools: Democratizing practice* (pp. 1–19). Norwood, MA: Christopher-Gordon.

Tang, J. (2013). Pragmatic functions of hedges and politeness principles. *International Journal of Applied Linguistics & English Literature, 2*(2), 155–160. Retrieved from www.ijalel.org/pdf/305.pdf

Wilkins-Canter, E. A. (1997). The nature and effectiveness of feedback given by cooperating teachers to student teachers. *Teacher Educator, 32*(4), 235–250. Retrieved from http://www.tandfonline.com/loi/utte20#.VaNgrPnvmPI

Yule, G. (1996). *Pragmatics.* Oxford, UK: Oxford University Press.

Zepeda, S. J. (2012). *Instructional supervision: Applying tools and concepts* (3rd ed.). New York: Routledge.

Zepeda, S. J. (2013). *The principal as instructional leader: A practical handbook* (3rd ed.). New York: Routledge.

Zepeda, S. J. (2015). *Job-embedded professional development: Support, collaboration, and learning in schools.* New York: Routledge.

Zepeda, S. J., & Ponticell, J. A. (1998). At cross-purposes: What do teachers need, want, and get from supervision? *Journal of Curriculum and Supervision, 14*(1), 68–87. Retrieved from http://www.ascd.org/publications/jcs/archived-issues.aspx

6 Improvement Planning with the Underperforming Teacher

In this chapter ...

- Framework for Plan of Improvement
- Plans of Improvement
- Plan of Improvement Framework
- Support Personnel and Resources Needed for Plans of Improvement
- Monitoring Plans of Improvement
- Moving Forward

The difficult conversations continue in a very formal way with the initiation of a plan of improvement, also commonly referred to as a *plan of remediation*, a *professional development* or *improvement plan*, or a *plan of assistance*. In addition to the plan of improvement, documentation is included from a variety of sources that captures performance in the area(s) of weakness. Along with the plan of improvement, specific resources, timelines, and personnel supports are identified.

Although the teacher going on a plan of improvement has deficits in performance, the school leader has to be careful not to fall into the trap of deficit thinking in which the teacher has to be "fixed." It's not the teacher; it's the performance (classroom instruction, classroom routines, and student management) or negative attitudes (disruptive interruption of school focus, culture, norms) or, possibly, attention to fulfilling contractual obligations (coming to school and arriving on time). However, a plan of improvement, depending on the severity of the issues identified and the teacher's progress toward remediating weaknesses, can lead to a recommendation of non-renewal or termination; legal considerations abound (see Chapter 8).

Nolan and Hoover (2011) share that "remediation ... is simply the right thing to do" (p. 300) and, from an organizational perspective, engaging teachers in the remediation process sends two very strong messages: "First, poor teaching performance is not acceptable. Second, the district is prepared to help teachers improve their performance and will work hard at doing so" (p. 300). It takes courage to write a formal plan of improvement (Eller & Eller, 2012; Fuhr, 1990, 1996; Jackson, 1997).

A few notes about non-renewal and termination: in Chapter 8 (written by Ann Blankenship), termination and non-renewal are examined. However, it is important to examine the differences between the two terms in concept and in theory, to understand the differences between teacher termination and non-renewal. While the result may be the same, the process is notably different. During a contract term or when a teacher has an automatically renewing contract (such as might be the case if the teacher is tenured), a teacher may be terminated only for cause. What constitutes a permissible cause for termination is governed by state law and varies somewhat from state to state; however, incompetency, insubordination, failure to obtain or maintain the proper licensure, and reduction in force generally are included as legal grounds for dismissal. When a teacher is terminated for cause during a contract term, he or she is entitled to due process, including notice, a hearing, and any additional protections provided for by state law.

When a teacher is approaching the end of his or her contract period and does not have the legal expectation of continued employment (as with tenure or the equivalent), the school district may choose to renew the teacher's contract or notify the teacher of non-renewal. Under contract law, a school district is not required to provide due process protections or grounds for termination for teachers who are non-renewed. However, it is important to note that many states have chosen to adopt some protections for teachers in this circumstance. These teachers may be entitled to some sort of explanation for the non-renewal and/ or some sort of appeals process. It is important that every school administrator be familiar with the termination and non-renewal procedures in his or her state.

Framework for Plan of Improvement

Through data and firsthand knowledge of a teacher's performance, the school leader needs to know when to move a teacher from informal supports to a more formal approach that becomes official because (1) clear evidence from one or more artifacts and evidence illustrate that a teacher has deficiencies in performance, and (2) informal supports have not been effective in remediating the areas of deficiency. The answer to the following question should be the litmus test: Would I want my child to be in this teacher's classroom for a full year? Moving to a formal plan of improvement is time consuming; the process relies on ongoing monitoring and the resolve that the teacher has to improve or face the consequences that could include termination or non-renewal. When a principal observes consistent problems and patterns of behavior that interfere with student learning, it is time to move toward a formal plan of improvement.

Ratcheting Consequences

A formal plan of improvement increases the consequences for a teacher who has not been able to address issues that have surfaced and for whom there is concrete data to support moving to a plan of improvement. Data are stable and are derived, in part, from the overall teacher evaluation system (see Chapter 2). Data and evidence are collected through a variety of sources that might include the following:

- **Classroom observations**: Formal and informal observations allow the principal to see the teacher's performance firsthand. Feedback has been shared with the teacher orally and in writing. Conversations and observation summaries include targeted areas for growth, and written commentary includes these areas that have been shared with the teacher during post-observation conferences.
- **Student and parent complaints**: Ineffective teachers come in contact with students on a daily basis, and they often interact with parents regarding their child's progress. The school leader follows up with teachers related to this feedback and engages teachers in conversations about the issues. This follow-up can take a variety of forms, including classroom observations, the examination of student work samples, test and quiz results, and discipline

referrals. These measures are undertaken so leaders can further their understanding of the issues to be able to provide guidance, link resources to support the teacher, and enlist building and system personnel such as instructional and/or content coaches and master teachers.

- **Data**: Value-added measures (growth measures) and other data routinely collected and that can be analyzed are another source of information to help frame strengths and weaknesses. Value-added measures link effects that individual teachers have on student learning using tests (see Chapter 2). Other data could also include pre- and post-test results and data from real-time software platforms that allow teachers and leaders to engage in progress monitoring. Through progress monitoring, teachers can adjust instruction so that changes reflect student needs. The leader can engage the teacher in conversations that reflect data and then address the planning and changes in practice that are or are not occurring.

- **Observations of teachers fulfilling their duties and responsibilities**: Patterns often emerge about a teacher's performance in their interactions and work habits with other adults. For example, leaders attend grade-level or team meetings and can see firsthand how teachers interact, how they work together, and whether a team member is hindering progress toward meeting goals. Some observable patterns might give rise to concern about a teacher:

  - Does the teacher have an inordinate number of absentee days, habitually arrive late, or habitually depart early?
  - Does the teacher miss team meetings?
  - Does the teacher fail to return parent calls or respond to emails?
  - Is the teacher overtly harsh, critical, and always on the attack with colleagues, students, parents, and others within the school or its system?

The conversations are more difficult when a formal plan of improvement is being developed. Honest feedback has to be direct, and the message must be clear that underperformance in and out of the classroom is not acceptable. Sugar-coating the conversation with hedging techniques (see Chapter 5) will not hide the elephant in the room—the underperforming teacher. More than likely, teachers in close physical proximity already are keenly aware of the issues the teacher is experiencing.

Union groups are very clear on their stance on plans of improvement. School systems and unions have more than likely come to formal terms of agreement regarding teacher improvement plans. There are legal ramifications associated with procedures, timelines, and the monitoring requirements. A teacher who is going to be non-renewed may or may not have legal recourse. For example, a first-year teacher does not have to be provided with cause for non-renewal; however, a tenured teacher with four or more years must be given cause, the right to a hearing, and other legal and procedural requirements dictated by state or accreditation agencies (see Chapter 8).

Given what we know about teacher effectiveness (see Chapter 1) and effective teaching (see Chapter 3), underperforming teachers really can no longer hide or be ignored by school leaders. It is the principal's duty to address and then confront teachers who do not meet expectations related to subject matter knowledge (Stronge, 2010), planning for instruction (Coe, Aloisio, Higgins, & Major, 2014), fidelity in the uses of high-yield instructional strategies (Marzano, Frontier, & Livingston, 2011), assessment (Stronge, 2010), a conducive learning environment (Stronge, Ward, Tucker, & Hindman, 2008), and maintaining effective patterns of communication with students and parents (Cornett-DeVito & Worley, 2005).

Plans of Improvement

Intent

For an underperforming teacher struggling in or out of the classroom, regardless of the magnitude of the struggle or the issues, the intent of any plan of improvement should be the growth and development of the teacher. The school leader needs to hold positive intentions with the belief that a teacher can be supported through the rough terrain of making improvements. Anything less than this attitude is really deficit thinking and renders the teacher, figuratively speaking, with one foot in the door and the other foot out of the door. Tucker (2001) explains that a plan of improvement "reflects the school system's concern for its teachers' professional development... [and] helping each teacher do so is an integral part of an instructional leader's role" (p. 53). Both the principal and the teacher must be motivated to do whatever it takes to resolve issues. An issue that goes unchecked has the potential to snowball, becoming larger and more acute.

Getting to Growth

The New York City Department of Education, Division of Teaching and Learning (n.d.), offers best practices that promote growth and communication between teachers and evaluators while creating and implementing a teacher improvement plan (TIP):

- **Communicate**: Let your teachers know that you're ready to listen, learn, and engage in a professional conversation through the TIP process throughout the school year.
- **Collaborate**: Invite teachers to reflect on their own teaching practice and evidence of student learning to identify areas of improvement and bring these ideas to the first TIP meeting. During that meeting, discuss and identify the action steps to achieve improvement in these areas, resources and support for those steps, the timeline, and how progress will be measured and assessed. In subsequent TIP meetings, discuss progress observed and next steps for the TIP improvement areas.
- **Check in frequently**: Ensure that the identified resources and support systems specified in the TIP are made available to the teacher. Also, invite the teacher to share ongoing progress with you.

(p. 1)

Leaders are asked to look within themselves to reflect on why they entered education—hopefully, to make a difference. In the instance of the underperforming teacher, morally and ethically, the focus is on the adult learner who needs support. To be a difference maker in the developmental lives of teachers necessitates that leaders commit to working with underperforming teachers. The plan of improvement is not about the leader; rather, the plan is about the teacher.

Herman (1993) reported that ineffective teachers found that plans of improvement worked only if they were motivated and supported, concluding that "from the practical application of effective strategies, administrators will need to recognize and deal with their own feelings of frustration and impatience as teachers struggle to improve" (p. 12). Teachers need and want the principal to be a visible presence in their instructional lives, and teachers need to be affirmed along the way to improvement (Zepeda & Ponticell, 1998; Ponticell & Zepeda, 2004).

Table 6.1 Considerations for Improvement Planning for Underperforming Teachers

- The experience level of the teacher
- The conceptual level of the teacher (new teacher, veteran teacher, teacher with experience who is now being asked to teach new skills or a new curriculum or to address different learners)
- The level of willingness on the part of the teacher (does not want to improve; is blinded by his or her weaknesses; cannot improve)
- The willingness of the principal to work with the underperforming teacher
- The context of the school, including culture, norms of collegiality, and trust
- The stance of the union or bargaining unit
- The history of supervision, evaluation, professional development, and the types of support given in the past to struggling teachers

Meeting a Teacher's Needs

There are factors that should be considered while thinking about the underperforming teacher:

- The severity of the underperformance: Severity dictates the urgency behind all plans of improvement.
- The timing of the underperformance: No time is ever good, but it is amazing how teacher performance dips immediately after the assignment of a summative rating for the year, with only a month left before the summer begins. Underperformance can occur at any time during the year.

Table 6.1 presents some ideas to consider as you think about underperformance and the plan of improvement. These same ideas will be referenced later in this chapter because they can help the principal think through the types of support underperforming teachers need.

Teacher Involvement in Improvement Planning

Conventional wisdom tells us that people resist change, especially when a plan of improvement will specify the deficiencies that must be addressed as well as identify and elaborate targeted changes that must occur within a specific time period. In Chapter 4, the responses of the teacher who has been identified as underperforming were discussed, and in Chapter 5, the types of conversations, including a focus on difficult ones, were examined.

For a plan of improvement to be approached with a sense of commitment, the teacher and the principal must be able to work as a team so that deficiencies can be diminished through sustained efforts to improve on the part of the teacher. Sometimes the cooperative efforts of the teacher and the principal are easier said than done.

Essentially, in a plan of improvement, the principal, as an agent for the school and system and an advocate for doing what's in the best interest of children, is asking underperforming teachers to make changes in some aspect about their practices or behaviors or both. Change can create new and exciting opportunities for some teachers, whereas for others change is met with resistance and anxiety (Fink & Stoll, 2005; Fullan, 2013). Regardless of resistance, anxiety, or even angst, "the heart of improvement lies in changing teaching and learning practices in thousands and thousands of classrooms" (Levin & Fullan, 2008, p. 289); however, Slavin (2005) reports that "it only takes one organizational development expert to change a light bulb, but the light bulb has to want to change" (p. 8). Plans of improvement, if they are to be effective, need to include very specific information to frame what needs to be communicated to an underperforming teacher.

Plan of Improvement Framework

It is in the plan of improvement where very specific and targeted goals are offered. Although there are differences across systems and states and requirements vary by policy and bargaining agreements with unions, most plans of improvement include as baseline the information found in Table 6.2.

Because every school system has its own way of communicating information, the leader is encouraged to become familiar with the types of formal documentation, policies, and procedures for developing a formal plan of improvement. The principal needs to be in a position to offer assistance and, at the same time, to take corrective actions beyond the plan of improvement if the teacher has not made progress.

Table 6.3 presents how the information would look in form fashion.

In Chapter 9, a completed plan of improvement is offered to support the leader in examining a totality of evidence related to an underperforming teacher.

Table 6.2 Essential Components of a Plan of Improvement

Section I: Area of Concern
• Identification of the problem or areas of concern that must improve: The description should also include artifacts that chronicle a timeline of the areas of concern.   • Processes to communicate the problem or areas of concern to the teacher both orally and in writing.
Section II: Objective and Goals for Improvement
• Statement of the objectives and goals for improvement.
Section III: Strategies to Meet Improvement
• Specific strategies and/or procedures, with the end in mind: Specific teacher behaviors must be indicated, with expected levels of performance included.
Section IV: Support and Resources
• Resources offered to assist the teacher with associated timelines.   • Documentation of progress toward the goals of improvement: Both the teacher and the principal (and others, in the case of a school system that includes other personnel in the process) must prepare reports on progress.
Section V: Timelines to Meet Areas of Concern
• Timelines, including when the plan begins, how frequently the teacher's performance will be evaluated, and who will do the evaluation(s).
Section VI: Monitoring the Plan
• Follow-up and monitoring strategies that will be used throughout the life of the plan of improvement.   • Documentation of the process of the plan of improvement, including meetings with the teacher, strategies offered, progress (or lack of progress) made.   • The types of processes that will follow if progress is not made on achieving the goals set forth on the plan of improvement.

Support Personnel and Resources Needed for Plans of Improvement

Because of the detail in the plan of improvement, the content of the plan becomes the compass to guide and focus all efforts by the principal and others. The supports, resources, and personnel that could be involved in the work with an underperforming teacher follow what has been indicated in the plan and, of course, follow what's possible given the context of the school and the resources available to the school from the system, local educational agencies, nearby school systems, colleges, and universities, and online materials.

Teachers on a plan of improvement need not go at improvement alone. In fact, supports would include key personnel such as the principal (or designee) who holds ultimate accountability for the quality of teachers and their

Table 6.3 Sample Plan of Improvement

Teacher _____ Date of Initial Meeting_____
Documentation of the process of the plan of remediation, including meetings with the teacher, strategies offered, progress (or lack of progress) made, resources offered to assist the teacher, and timelines.
Section I: Areas of Concern
Concern Area 1:
Description of Current Weakness:
Related Artifact and Evidence:
Concern Area 2:
Description of Current Weakness:
Related Artifact and Evidence:
Concern Area 3:
Description of Current Weakness:
Related Artifact and Evidence

Section II: Objective and Goals for Improvement
Area 1 Objectives and Goals for Improvement:
Area 2 Objectives and Goals for Improvement:
Area 3 Objectives and Goals for Improvement:
Section III: Strategies to Meet Improvement
Area 1 Strategies to Meet Improvement:
Area 2 Strategies to Meet Improvement:
Area 3 Strategies to Meet Improvement:
Section IV: Support and Resources
Area 1 Support and Resources:
Provided by:
Area 2 Support and Resources:
Provided by:
Area 3 Support and Resources:
Provided by:
Section V: Timelines to Meet Areas of Concern
Area 1 Timeline to Meet Areas of Concern:
Area 2 Timeline to Meet Areas of Concern:
Area 3 Timeline to Meet Areas of Concern:

continued…

Table 6.3 continued

Section VI: Monitoring the Plan			
Area of Concern	**Supports and Resources**	**Provided by/Date**	**Progress Toward Improvement**
Area 1:			
Area 2:			
Area 3:			

This plan spans from *(list dates)* _____ to
_____. Written and oral feedback will be given formally on *(list dates)*
_____, _____, and _____.
Principal's Signature _____ Date_____
Teacher's Signature _____ Date_____

Adapted from Zepeda, 2012, 2013

effectiveness with delivering the instructional program according to content and the standards, maintaining a learning environment conducive to student learning, and ensuring assessments match learning objectives.

Many school systems have instructional and/or content coaches in key areas such as literacy and mathematics. Some schools have instructional interventionists who work within a key area (e.g., math). In addition, many schools have teachers who serve as mentors to early-career teachers; high schools are staffed with department chairs; middle schools often have lead teachers.

Support personnel are essential to provide extra help for all teachers. These key personnel do not hold authority to evaluate teachers; rather, they mentor and coach underperforming teachers, focusing on the improvement of practice. There are also support personnel from the central office who serve as curriculum specialists, system-wide content coaches, and instructional coaches who rotate across the system.

It is not uncommon to have within school systems or even at the site level assistance teams that work with underperforming teachers. The principal would appoint the team, monitor the types of support the assistance team would provide, and then follow up with the administrative duties of evaluating results based solely on the underperforming teacher's performance. The principal would communicate with the assistance team in a very open forum with the underperforming teacher present. Caution is offered in that it is only what the principal observes or collects data about that is included in an evaluation. Processes and procedures would need to be codified and unfold according to local policies, agreements with unions, and the like.

Support personnel would engage in very specific efforts to support growth and development. Supports could include professional learning through

- peer coaching and informal classroom observations;
- mentoring;
- focused professional development;
- analyzing videotaped lessons;
- participating in district-wide support programs (induction and mentoring);
- observing in the classrooms of exceptional teachers who can model effective teaching skills;
- joining a book study group;
- participating in online programs such as MOOCS [Massive Open Online Courses], webinars, and discussion groups related to grade levels or subject/content areas;
- studying student work samples and test data; and engaging in action research

(Zepeda, 2015)

Resources are the tangible items that a school can provide—for example, books, study guides, and electronic repositories run by the system or state department of education that curates documents that illustrate best practices. Online resources are available as well, such as Facebook and Pinterest. Buildings often share resources, and the central office typically houses resources. Local educational agencies that serve systems clustered in geographic areas are also a great source to tap for resources, as are local colleges and universities. The reader is encouraged to look deep within the site to tap school personnel and the resources available to support underperforming teachers.

Monitoring Plans of Improvement

Attention to detail is the foundation to monitoring a plan of improvement. The plan of improvement is specific and includes the areas of concern, targeted improvements, and detail to timelines, especially when improvement must be made and to what degree of improvement. Essentially, the principal needs to know whether the plan is working, whether activities and strategies of the plan of improvement yielded changes in practice, and what modifications need to be made to ensure progress keeps moving forward.

Monitoring could include classroom observations to see the degree to which instructional improvements are being made, examination of student work samples to see the evidence of student progress on key content-specific areas, tracking of discipline referrals, and the like. Frequent meetings with an underperforming teacher on a plan of improvement are critical, and feedback on progress is essential. Typically, there is a beginning, middle, and end to a plan of improvement, and meetings and feedback should follow the trail of these time markers.

A lack of oversight and supervision of an underperforming teacher can compromise the intent of the plan of improvement—to support the growth of a teacher who is underperforming—and thus negatively impact students and perhaps the school. Both written and verbal feedback need to be provided in the form of a progress report related to the goals, objectives, and areas of concern that have been identified.

Moving Forward

The stakes are high for a building-level leader and for the underperforming teacher on a plan of improvement. Even an underperforming teacher may one day become an exceptionally strong teacher, so difficult conversations should be viewed as having the potential to make the school a better place instead of a means to put a Band-Aid on a particular problem. It is up to the principal to consider carefully the most appropriate methods to help guide an underperforming teacher to exemplary teaching practices, based on that teacher's particular needs and personality.

The underperforming teacher must want to be in engaged in the process and improve; otherwise, the efforts of the principal and other support personnel will be fruitless. It is possible that some teachers may resist engaging in what needs to be accomplished to improve their own performance. In the final analysis, improvement rests squarely on the shoulders of the underperforming teacher. Without sufficient progress, tough decisions will need to be made about the status of an underperforming teacher (see Chapter 9).

Before a final decision is reached about whether to recommend a teacher's contract renewal, many more areas need to be examined, including the leader's skills, the barriers that the principal or the system might experience related to confronting underperforming teachers (see Chapter 7), the possible legal issues surrounding the work with an underperforming teacher (see Chapter 8), and the moral and ethical considerations involved with working with underperforming teachers (see Chapter 9).

References

Coe, R., Aloisio, C., Higgins, S., & Major, L. E. (2014). *What makes great teaching? Review of the underpinning research.* London: Sutton Trust. Retrieved from http://www.suttontrust.com/researcharchive/great-teaching

Cornett-DeVito, M. M., & Worley, D. W. (2005). A front row seat: A phenomenological investigation of learning disabilities. *Communication Education, 54*(4), 312–333. doi:10.1080/03634520500442178

Eller, J. F., & Eller, S. A. (2012). Working productively with difficult and resistant staff. *Principal,* 28–30. Retrieved from www.naesp.org/SeptOct12

Fink, D., & Stoll, L. (2005). Educational change: Easier said than done. In A. Hargreaves (Ed.), *Extending educational change* (pp. 17–41). Netherlands: Springer.

Fuhr, D. (1990). Supervising the marginal teacher: Here's how. *National Association of Elementary Teachers, 9*(2), 1–4. Retrieved from http://www.eric.ed.gov:80/PDFS/ED324825.pdf

Fuhr, D. (1996). *No margin for error: Saving our schools from borderline teachers.* Dubuque, IA: Kendall/Hunt.

Fullan, M. (2013). Introduction. In M. Fullan (Ed.), *The challenge of change* (pp. 3–8). Thousand Oaks, CA: Corwin.

Herman, D. (1993). Remediating marginal teachers: What makes plans of assistance work? *Oregon School Study Council Report, 34*(1), 1–12. Retrieved from http://www.eric.ed.gov:80/PDFS/ED364935.pdf

Jackson, C. M. (1997). Assisting marginal teachers: A training model. *Principal, 77*(1), 28–30. Retrieved from http://www.naesp.org

Levin, B., & Fullan, M. (2008). Learning about system renewal. *Educational Management Administration & Leadership, 36*(2), 289–303. doi:10.1177/1741143207087778

Marzano, R. J., Frontier, T., & Livingston, D. (2011). *Effective supervision: Supporting the art and science of teaching.* Alexandria, VA: Association for Supervision and Curriculum Development.

New York City Department of Education, Division of Teaching and Learning. (n.d.). *At a glance: Best practices for teacher improvement plans.* New York: Author. Retrieved from http://schools.nyc.gov/default.htm

Nolan, J., Jr., & Hoover, L. A. (2011). *Teacher supervision and evaluation: Theory into practice* (3rd ed.). Hoboken, NJ: John Wiley & Sons.

Ponticell, J. A., & Zepeda, S. J. (2004). Confronting well-learned lessons in supervision and evaluation. *The NASSP Bulletin, 88*(639), 43–59. doi:10.1177/019263650408863905

Slavin, R. E. (2005). Sand, bricks, and seeds: School change strategies and readiness for reform. In D. Hopkins (Ed.), *The practice and theory of school improvement* (pp. 265–279). Netherlands: Springer.

Stronge, J. H. (2010). *Effective teachers = student achievement: What the research says.* Larchmont, NY: Eye on Education.

Stronge, J. H., Ward, T. J., Tucker, P. D., & Hindman, J. L. (2008). What is the relationship between teacher quality and student achievement? An exploratory study. *Journal of Personnel Evaluation in Education, 20(3–4),* 165–184. doi: 10.1007/s11092-008-9053-z

Tucker, P. (2001). Helping struggling teachers. *Educational Leadership, 58*(5), 52–55. Retrieved from http://web.ebscohost.com

Zepeda, S. J. (2012). *Instructional supervision: Applying tools and concepts* (3rd ed.). New York: Routledge.

Zepeda, S. J. (2013). *The principal as instructional leader: A practical handbook* (3rd ed.). New York: Routledge.

Zepeda, S. J. (2015). *Job-embedded professional development: Support, collaboration, and learning in schools.* New York: Routledge.

Zepeda, S. J., & Ponticell, J. A. (1998). At cross-purposes: What do teachers need, want, and get from supervision? *Journal of Curriculum and Supervision, 14*(1), 68–87. Retrieved from http://www.ascd.org/publications/jcs/archived-issues.aspx

The Complexities Leaders Face in Working with Underperforming Teachers

7

Teacher evaluation often creates stress for both teachers and leaders, and the "political reform" associated with teacher evaluation "has arguably intensified conflicts already inherent in teacher evaluation , [and] such tensions are likely to increase" according to Conley and Glasman (2008, p. 68). The complexities are exacerbated for leaders while working with underperforming teachers to the extent that many principals "tolerate ineffective [teachers] because they know that confronting them will be cognitively demanding, emotionally draining, and physically exhausting" (McEwan, 2005, p. 120). It is indeed demanding work, especially for leaders who might be new to a building and discover that underperforming teachers are employed there (Zepeda, 2012, 2013).

Kelley and Maslow (2005) offer a spectrum of conditions that could possibly compromise a principal's ability to assert leadership related to evaluating and working with underperforming and, perhaps, all teachers:

1 Limitations in supervisor competency;
2 Inadequate time for observation and feedback;
3 Lack of teacher/administration understanding and acceptance;
4 Narrow conceptions of teaching;
5 Lack of clarity about evaluation criteria;
6 Classroom observations that are subject to evaluator preferences;
7 Conflicts between the roles of evaluator as instructional leader and staff supervisor; and
8 Principals' lack of content-specific knowledge, resulting in evaluation feedback that focuses on general behaviors, such as delivery, rather than on content-specific pedagogy.

(p. 1)

These ideas and others presented in this chapter are worthy of exploration, because leaders need the courage and resolve to work with underperforming teachers.

Preparation and Background of the Evaluator

Not all preparation leading to the principalship or a supervisory position is equal. As Fuhr (1996) reports, "Unfortunately, few schools of higher education prepare school administrators for the challenges of remediating marginal performers" (pp. xi–xii). More recently, Range, Duncan, Scherz, and Haines (2012) offered that the "capacity of preservice and practicing principals must be developed so that they are prepared to be instructional leaders equipped with the skills necessary to address ineffective teachers" (p. 316). Although most preparation programs include a basic course in instructional supervision and/or teacher evaluation, it is doubtful that much time, depth, or breadth about the underperforming teacher is afforded to these topics. Likewise, school law courses deal with the procedural aspects of due process, termination, and non-renewal. However, working with underperforming teachers requires sustained efforts and skills in such areas as conducting classroom observations, engaging in difficult conversations, and applying principles of adult learning, motivation, and psychology.

School leaders must have command of a new language—the language of teaching, learning, and assessment. Constant changes in standards (e.g., Common Core State Standards, Next-Generation Science Standards), the proliferation of digital tools to promote "connected" classrooms and instruction, and high-stakes testing requirements necessitate a strong knowledge in curriculum and instruction. Moreover, these changes require the leader to have a strong background in professional learning to support teachers as they grapple with implementing new standards and content. To engage in conversations, school leaders will need to know what effective teaching looks like and to be able to describe what students would be doing as the fabric of teaching unfolds in the classroom.

Principals can take a proactive stance in their own development by consulting with other building-level leaders, enrolling in specialty courses that deal with supporting teachers with issues, engaging in professional development, reading books, and asking the central office to provide ongoing training and support to assist with learning the skills needed to work with underperforming teachers.

Shifts in Evaluation

Teacher evaluation systems look very different today than they did a few years ago. Most states have tightly wound rules and regulations that dictate processes, strict timelines, and electronic reporting systems that cull and then link the results of student testing to a teacher's overall effectiveness (see Chapter 2). The complexities of new teacher evaluation systems have caused a sense of disequilibrium for leaders who have to focus more time on the logistics of the teacher evaluation systems versus focusing time on working with individual teachers.

The research of Range et al. (2012) illustrated that principals have become frustrated with the time that the evaluation process consumes. In a similar vein, Sartain, Stoelinga, and Brown (2011) reported that 15% of the principals in their study were resistant to the new evaluation system because they believed they "'just knew' teachers' abilities, … and these principals perceived that the evaluation system had no impact on instructional practice … They also placed teacher evaluation at the low end of priorities compared with their other responsibilities" (p. 39).

Struggles Enacting Evaluation

Psychological Stressors

Working with underperforming teachers can be extremely stressful—"cognitively demanding, emotionally draining, and physically exhausting" (McEwan, 2005,

p. 120). Bridges (1990) states that this work evokes "powerful emotions—fear, self-doubt, anger, and guilt" (p. 57). No administrator wants to have to confront a teacher for subpar performance. There are the human factors involved. For example, the teacher might very well be a good person and have experienced tragic personal events that, unfortunately, have affected performance. However, underperformance in and out of the classroom must be confronted.

The principal who confronts underperforming teachers might feel vulnerable, especially if this is a new school for the principal. The new principal (or even the veteran principal new to a building assignment) has not had the opportunity to establish credibility and trust with the faculty. Bridges (1992) speaks of the "criticism" factor, which is a two-way street for both the principal and the teacher: "The most important personal factor is the deeply seated human desire to avoid conflict and unpleasantness which often accompany criticism from others" (p. 20).

Kaye (2004) reports another potential conflict in which teachers and administrators might have to choose sides—the side of the administrator who has confronted underperformance and the side of some teachers who want to support other teachers regardless. Kaye describes such conflict like this: "The implementation of compensatory and covert disciplinary responses to marginality by administrators has placed teachers and teaching in a context in which the conflict between rightness and fairness is not easily resolved" (pp. 254–255).

Role Conflict and Relationships with Teachers

In Chapter 2, the tug-of-war between the formative and summative side of evaluation can create role confusion for school leaders who must support teachers and then render a summative rating at the end of the year. This tension is a perennial one that has endured with the belief that supervision and evaluation serve two purposes and thus the two need to be separately enacted by different people. That opinion, held by many, is not very practical in schools under most staffing patterns because there are only so many certified people to supervise and evaluate in a building.

Some leaders have reservations about rating teachers for fear of the possible confrontation or backlash from the union. The safety net that surrounds teachers—fellow teachers who will complain about underperforming teachers privately in the leader's office but commiserate with the underperforming teacher in the hallways—often puts a leader at odds with the faculty.

Lack of Support from the Central Office

Although it might seem like a lonely journey for a principal working with an underperforming teacher, there is a need for others to be involved. The underperforming teacher is not easy to confront without the support and backing of the central office (Bridges, 1990; Fuhr, 1996). Blacklock (2002) warns:

> The principal can't do it alone. Making decisions of this magnitude, developing an improvement process that is fair for the teacher, and remaining focused on improvement until the evidence is unequivocal requires the full support and involvement of central office administrators.
>
> (p. 27)

Support is critically important especially in instances where remediation efforts do not yield favorable results. Once a principal detects and substantiates that a teacher is underperforming, the central office (e.g., director of personnel; director of elementary, secondary, or high school education; assistant superintendent) should be consulted to gain perspective, garner support for confrontation, learn procedures, and glean any other information that will help the principal confront and work with an underperforming teacher.

Perceptions About Present and Past Site Leadership

There is not a single principal who likes the idea of having underperforming teachers present in the school. Generally speaking, teachers who are underperforming did not just suddenly become ineffective. The markers of underperformance have more than likely been evident for some time but have been kept off the proverbial radar. Fuhr (1996) reports that most underperforming teachers learn to "become experts at putting on a 'show' before the evaluator" (p. 22). A principal might fear that discovering an underperforming teacher who has worked in the building for some time might cast a shadow on the principal's credibility. Many principals believe that if such a teacher is discovered, the principals will be viewed negatively by their immediate supervisors.

A principal who is new to a building and discovers a marginal teacher might be in a difficult situation by bringing this information to light, especially if the former principal was revered by the faculty and the central office administration.

This would be especially true if the former principal now occupies a central office position. Once an underperforming teacher is placed on a plan of improvement (see Chapter 6), news will spread. Fellow teachers could doubt the accuracy of the principal's assessment of the underperforming teacher. However, principals who do not confront an underperforming teacher face losing credibility with the faculty. Competent teachers really do not want to work alongside underperforming teachers who have been able to stay off the radar. The perspectives of Fuhr (1996) add to this discussion:

> Principals don't like to talk about the marginal or incompetent teacher, or admit that such teachers are in their schools. The reason is obvious. It makes the management team look bad. Meanwhile, parents, students and the effective teachers wonder why marginal teachers are allowed to continue teaching without something being done to improve their skills.
>
> (p. 1)

Organization of Work

School Culture

Allensworth (2012) reports that "[s]chools that show the largest improvements are those where teachers work collectively on improving instruction, and where school leadership is inclusive and focused on instruction" (p. 30). Perceptions about supervising and evaluating teachers are embedded into the culture of the school (see Chapter 2). Here are a few questions to help you reflect on the culture, norms, and climate in which supervision and evaluation unfold:

1   Do teachers believe you enter their classrooms with the intent of helping them improve their instructional practices?
2   Do feedback conferences and other work associated with the interactions between the evaluator and teacher promote growth, development, interaction, fault-free problem-solving, and a commitment to building teacher capacity?
3   How often do you engage teachers in conversations about teaching and learning beyond classroom observations? In other words, are the conversations about teaching and learning part of a larger strategy to help teachers think about their work in classrooms with students?

The responses to these questions should serve as a compass for leaders to examine their supervisory and evaluative practices in addition to the types of supports that are offered to teachers. The answers to these questions point to the culture of a school and the care and concern that leaders hold for teachers.

A school leader is one who does more than just merely observe teachers in the classroom setting once or twice a year. The school leadership enacts myriad roles in promoting growth and learning for teachers that, hopefully, leads to growth and learning for students.

Time Constraints

In a 2009 Wallace Foundation study, time as it relates to the work of the principal was explored. The data showed that principals spend *about 70%* of their time on management functions that include such concerns as student discipline, student supervision, employee discipline, office work/preparation, building management, dealing with parents, and attending management meetings. In stark contrast, principals spent *30%* of their time on the instructional program, including such activities as working with students, observing teachers, conducting classroom visits, providing feedback to teachers, and participating in professional development.

Thirty percent of a workday or workweek just is not sufficient: The tension is that principals know they need to spend time with the instructional program, but there are only so many hours in a day or a week. In other words, there are many duties and responsibilities that leaders need to attend to in addition to the instructional program. In a similar vein, May and Supovitz (2011) report principals dedicate around 18% of their time to the area of instruction and curriculum and approximately 3% of their time on teacher evaluation.

The amount of time a supervisor will spend working with an underperforming teacher is immense. Fuhr (1996) writes, "Managing the marginal teachers will involve extra time needed for reading reports, planning, consulting with experts, and arranging conferences" (p. 8). More time, however, will be spent observing the teacher informally and formally and following up with feedback.

Depending on the specifics of the plan of improvement, the principal could also have other tasks, such as arranging for the teacher to observe other teachers, arranging for the teacher to participate in professional development, and then committing the outcomes of these efforts to writing. The principal will spend a great deal of time communicating not only with the underperforming teacher but also with central office personnel.

The complexities that leaders face when dealing with underperforming teachers are context specific, and each site will have its own set of circumstances that could cause the leader to experience difficulty beyond the obvious; underperforming teachers must improve, period. Chapter 8 examines legal issues, and Chapter 9 examines moral and ethical decisions. These are the tough decisions that leaders must make.

References

Allensworth, E. (2012). Want to improve teaching? Create collaborative, supportive schools. *American Educator, 36*(3), 30–31. Retrieved from http://eric.ed.gov/?id=EJ986682

Blacklock, K. (2002). Dealing with an incompetent teacher. *Principal, 81*(4), 26–28. Retrieved from http://www.naesp.org/principal-archives

Bridges, E. M. (1990). *Managing the incompetent teacher* (2nd ed.). Eugene, OR: ERIC.

Bridges, E. M. (1992). *The incompetent teacher: Managerial responses*. London: Falmer Press.

Conley, S., & Glasman, N. S. (2008). Fear, the school organization, and teacher evaluation. *Educational Policy, 22*(1), 63–85. doi: 10.1177/0895904807311297

Fuhr, D. (1996). *No margin for error: Saving our schools from borderline teachers*. Dubuque, IA: Kendall/Hunt.

Kaye, E. B. (2004). Turning the tide on marginal teaching. *Journal of Curriculum and Supervision, 19*(3), 234–258. Retrieved from http://www.ascd.org/publications/jcs/archived-issues.aspx

Kelley, C., & Maslow, V. (2005). *The effects of teacher evaluation on equity and system change in large, diverse high schools*. Paper presented at the April 2005 conference of the American Research Association, Montreal, Canada.

May, H., & Supovitz, J. A. (2011). The scope of principal efforts to improve instruction. *Educational Administration Quarterly, 47*(2), 332–352. doi: 10.1177/0013161X10383411

McEwan, E. (2005). *How to deal with teachers who are angry, troubled, exhausted, or just plain confused*. Thousand Oaks, CA: Corwin.

Range, B. G., Duncan, H. E., Scherz, S. D., & Haines, C. A. (2012). School leaders' perceptions about incompetent teachers: Implications for supervision and evaluation. *NASSP Bulletin, 96*(4), 302–322. doi: 10.1177/0192636512459554

Sartain, L., Stoelinga, S., & Brown, E. (2011). *Rethinking teacher evaluation in Chicago: Lessons learned from classroom observations, principal-teacher conferences, and district implementation*. Chicago: Consortium on Chicago School Research: University of Chicago, Urban Education Institute. Retrieved from https://ccsr.uchicago.edu/publications/rethinking-teacher-evaluation-chicago-lessons-learned-classroom-observations-principal

Wallace Foundation. (2009). *Assessing the effectiveness of school Leaders: New directions and new processes*. A Wallace Foundation Perspective, 7–8. New York,

NY: Author. Retrieved from http://www.wallacefoundation.org/knowledge-center/school-leadership/principal-evaluation/Documents/Assessing-the-Effectiveness-of-School-Leaders.pdf

Zepeda, S. J. (2012). *Instructional supervision: Applying tools and concepts* (3rd ed.). Larchmont, NY: Eye on Education.

Zepeda, S. J. (2013). *The principal as instructional leader: A practical handbook* (3rd ed.). New York: Routledge.

8 Keeping Classroom Issues out of the Courtroom

Legal Principles for Confronting Underperforming Teachers

by Ann Elizabeth Blankenship[1]

> *In this chapter ...*
>
> - Competence and Incompetence—Legally Defining Elusive Concepts
> - Why Underperformance Is Overlooked
> - Due Process Requirements in Evaluation and Termination
> - Teacher Evaluations
> - Emerging Legal Issues Associated with Teacher Evaluations, Including Value-Added Models
> - Moving Toward Termination

Introduction[2]

In a public service field as large as education, with more than 3.5 million teachers instructing our nation's children, it is inevitable that some teachers will fail to meet acceptable performance standards. However, given the extensive research that links quality teaching to student achievement, schools cannot afford to have ineffectual teachers in the classroom (Darling-Hammond, 2000;

Fuhr, 1990; Hanushek, 1992; Hanushek & Rivkin, 2006). It is imperative for administrators to be able to identify teachers who are struggling or failing to meet expectations so that they can receive appropriate intervention or, when necessary, they can be removed.

This chapter discusses the legal issues that can arise when a teacher is underperforming. The first step in addressing the issue of underperformance is identifying the behavior. The first section of this chapter looks at the issue of teacher competence, how to identify underperforming teachers, and why so many administrators fail to identify underperforming teachers in formal evaluations. This section includes a brief discussion of the role of teachers' unions in this process and the evaluation process. Used properly, evaluation can be a powerful tool for both formative and summative purposes. This section discusses the constitutional due process requirements and state law issues that must be addressed when conducting an evaluation. The legal issues associated with teacher evaluations, including the use of value-added models (VAMs), are examined. The third section of this chapter addresses defamation issues that can arise from a negative teacher evaluation and how to avoid legal liability. The final section of this chapter discusses the procedural requirements that must be met to eliminate poor performance.

Each state and district has its own regulations and procedures for dealing with poor performance, and each case will have unique facts and circumstances. Therefore, this chapter should be seen as an introduction to the legal issues associated with underperforming teachers. Administrators are strongly encouraged to become familiar with the laws and regulations that apply in their specific state as well as district policies and procedures.

Competence and Incompetence— Legally Defining Elusive Concepts

Dealing with issues of teacher competence can be challenging for an administrator. Research indicates that there is a dramatic discrepancy between the number of incompetent teachers and the number of teachers who are identified as incompetent, or even unsatisfactory, in their teacher evaluations (Weisberg, Sexton, Mulhern, & Kelling, 2009). Although an estimate of the true number of incompetent teachers is difficult to make, scholars estimate that it ranges from 5% to 10% (Bridges, 1992). In a 2009 study of 12 urban school districts, fewer than 1% of teachers received unsatisfactory evaluations

(Weisberg et al., 2009). Thus, it appears that either evaluation systems or the school administrators implementing them are failing to identify poorly performing teachers. It is imperative that administrators accurately evaluate their teachers to identify teachers' strengths and weaknesses, provide appropriate teacher interventions, and ensure sufficient resource allocations for professional development, and that they build the proper documentation of incompetence for dismissal proceedings. To that end, this section provides administrators with the tools to identify poor performance in the classroom.

Why Underperformance Is Overlooked

To maintain quality instruction for students, it is imperative that administrators be able to properly assess teacher performance. The majority of teachers perform competently, if not exceptionally. However, there are teachers who are underperforming or even incompetent. The first step to identifying these teachers is to know how to define and to understand the differences between underperformance and incompetence.

The Underperforming Teacher

An underperforming, or marginal teacher, may be difficult to identify because his or her skill level falls between competent and incompetent (Lawrence, Vachon, Leake, & Leake, 2005). Lawrence et al. (2005) and Fuhr (1990) both note that underperforming teachers may be hard to spot because their performance is inconsistent. They often put forth more effort to get through their yearly evaluation but, for the rest of the year, do just enough to get by (Fuhr, 1990; Lawrence et al., 2005). While marginal teachers may be well-educated and credentialed, their behavior may not reflect their training. Lawrence et al. (2005) note that marginal teachers may be "unprepared, deficient in teaching skills, unable or unwilling to improve their teaching, have classroom management problems, have a negative attitude about the teaching profession, and have a high tardiness and absence rate" (p. 11). With the proper intervention, marginal teachers can improve their performance. However, without the proper attention, marginal teachers' performance will continue to be poor and could even deteriorate further.

The Incompetent Teacher

Incompetence, particularly when it is used as grounds for dismissal, may prove to be a challenging concept for administrators. A review of court rulings suggests that teacher incompetence is not determined by deficiencies in one area alone but instead is determined by multiple deficiencies (Rossow & Tate, 2003). Tigges (1965) noted:

> The incompetent teacher is rarely deficient in one respect alone; rather, incompetency seems to manifest itself in a pervasive pattern encompassing a multitude of sins and bringing in its wake disorganization, dissatisfaction, disharmony, and an atmosphere unproductive for the acquisition of knowledge or attainment of any other ancillary benefit.
>
> (p. 1102)

It is important to note that for purposes of making termination decisions, incompetence is defined by state law and therefore varies based on location.

Traditionally, teachers dismissed for incompetence would have a record of grievous misconduct. For example, in *Perez v. Commission on Professional Competence* (1983), the California Court of Appeals held that the school district's commission presented enough evidence to uphold the dismissal of Mr. Perez for incompetence from his position as a Spanish teacher. Evidence indicated that Mr. Perez failed to properly manage his class, demonstrated by students' tardiness and inattention, their taking siestas and talking in class, their open disdain for discipline, and their reading of unrelated material in class, culminating in an incident in which two students set a rug on fire in the classroom and Mr. Perez did nothing. In rendering its opinion, the court noted that *incompetence* is not a vague or uncertain term. It stated:

> It is a plain word and means not competent. Competent, in turn, means properly or well qualified; capable – adequate for the purpose, suitable; sufficient. Incompetency does not invoke subjective analysis of standards of morality or professionalism which vary from individual to individual dependent on time, circumstances or custom.
>
> (p. 396)

Therefore, as long as administrators rely on the state law or local policy regarding competent teaching practices and on the facts, administrators should be able to identify and to deal with incompetence.

However, even when states give general criteria for determining competence, it still could be unclear as to what acts serve as legitimate indicators of incompetence and how many specific instances the administrator must witness to persuade a ruling body that there was enough evidence of incompetence to warrant dismissal. This ambiguity could render an administrator uncertain about the strength of the dismissal, particularly if it is challenged in court (Bridges, 1992).

In an effort to address this ambiguity, a number of states have revised their dismissal and suspension statutes to include negative teacher evaluations in the definition of incompetency (or the like). For example, in 2011, Tennessee dramatically revised their teacher tenure and dismissal process. Under the new law, a teacher may be dismissed for receiving teaching evaluations that are below expectations or significantly below expectations. The increasing use of student test scores in teaching evaluations and, thus, high-stakes employment decisions raises a number of legal issues that will be discussed later in this chapter.

Managerial Concerns

Looking at the numbers, it may be difficult to understand how so many administrators fail to identify poor performance among their own teachers. In his seminal 1992 text, Bridges identified the three factors—two situational and one personal—that most greatly contribute to administrators' inclination to tolerate and protect, rather than confront, poor performance in the classroom. The situational factors include the legal employment rights of the teacher, or tenure status, and the complexities of the evaluation process itself. Bridges states that "the most important personal factor is the deeply seated human desire to avoid the conflict and unpleasantness which often accompany criticism of others" (Bridges, 1992, p. 20). Other researchers have identified additional aspects of evaluation systems that may prove particularly challenging: The structural system of evaluation systems themselves; lack of time and support for an evaluating administrator; an evaluator's personality characteristics (which could be both situational and/or personal, depending on the circumstances); and an administrator's lack of knowledge and/or skill in conducting evaluations (Painter, 2000; Tucker, 1997).

Bridges notes that a teacher's employment rights, particularly tenure status, may influence an administrator's willingness to accurately evaluate the teacher's performance (1992). Both tenure and teacher evaluations are discussed next.

Due Process Requirements in Evaluation and Termination

While the concept of tenure is most often associated with college and university faculty, similar employment protections are or have been available to elementary and secondary teachers in all 50 states (Blankenship, 2014). While some view tenure is a guarantee to lifetime employment, it is actually the "expectation and provision of job security through the guarantee of due process, generally following a probationary period" (Blankenship, 2014, p. 195). Tenure is a product of state, not federal, law so it looks different in each state. Teachers are granted tenure after a probationary period of 1 (Hawaii) to 7 (Ohio) years' teaching, with a majority of states granting tenure after only 3 years (Blankenship, 2014; Cohen & Walsh, 2010; Education Commission of the States, 2007). While some states require a record of satisfactory evaluations for teachers to be eligible for tenure, generally tenure is a right that is automatically granted after the expiration of the probationary period.

Due Process

Under the due process clause of the Fourteenth Amendment of the Constitution of the United States[3], an individual is entitled to due process of law before the state can infringe on the individual's right to life, liberty, or property.[4] At its most basic, procedural due process entitles an individual to notice of the charges (or reason for the negative action) and an opportunity to be heard by a neutral trier of fact. State law dictates the particular notice and hearing requirements. Often, states also offer a number of additional rights as part of their due process guarantee, including the right to be represented by an attorney, the right to subpoena witnesses and documents, and the right to appeal through administrative and/or court systems.

Tenured Teachers

In the 1972 case *Board of Regents of State College v. Roth*, the Supreme Court stated that the requirements of procedural due process apply when a teacher has been deprived of his or her property or liberty interests. A tenured teacher has a vested property interest in his or her job because he or she has a continued legal expectation of employment. Consequently, due process rights are naturally a part of tenure protections before a tenured teacher faces a negative employment action, including termination, suspension, or demotion. Each state sets statutory grounds for termination, which may include incompetency/poor performance, insubordination, willful neglect of duty, reduction in force, and failure to maintain proper licensure.[5]

Some grounds for dismissal are simpler than others for administrators to prove. For example, failure to obtain proper licensure or even insubordination is more objective and can be proven with limited documentation. However, termination for poor performance (incompetence, inefficiency, etc.) is more complicated because it involves an element of subjectivity. Traditionally, poor performance as a ground for dismissal (or other negative employment action) has been poorly defined in state law, forcing administrators to rely on piecemeal guidelines revealed in case law. With budget cuts and increased focus on accountability, administrators cannot afford to keep underperforming teachers in the classroom. Many states have addressed this issue by redefining incompetence, relying in part or wholly on teacher evaluations, streamlining the tenure and termination processes, and making changes to reduction-in-force procedures.

Probationary Teachers

During the probationary period, teachers are considered "at-will" employees and may be dismissed without cause at the end of any contract period unless otherwise prescribed by state law. Teachers are generally not entitled to due process during the probationary period.[6] However, a teacher's right to not have his or her reputation defamed is a constitutionally protected liberty interest; injury to reputation may negatively impact an individual's ability to secure future employment. If grounds for termination of a non-tenured teacher are made public, it may entitle that teacher to procedural due process. Publishing negative information about a teacher also can provide grounds for a defamation suit under state law, which is discussed in more detail later in this chapter.

Teacher Evaluations

Teacher evaluation is the most commonly used tool for identifying underperforming and incompetent teachers (see Chapter 2). It can be used to improve instruction for all teachers by identifying professional development needs, to identify poorly performing teachers and guide the mitigation process, and to justify the termination of incompetent teachers. The reform movement of the 1980s brought a lot of attention to teacher evaluation as a tool of accountability—a way to measure teacher effectiveness. Reform efforts focused on improving teaching and learning but also on improving the evaluation methods themselves. Before the reform movement, few states and localities had legislation directly addressing teacher evaluation. However, between 1983 and 1992 the number of states that had law specifically focused on evaluation rose from 20 to 38 (Veir & Dagley, 2002). While early efforts to legislate evaluation were at the state level, since the early 2000s, legislative efforts have been more focused at the local level. Therefore, depending on the state, the requirements of a teacher evaluation system may be laid out in the state law, local regulation, or both.

Purpose Versus Use of Teacher Evaluations

The purpose of an evaluation system and how the results are to be used also vary based on the state and should be set forth in either state law or local regulation. Knowing the stated purpose of the evaluation system and intended use of evaluations in a particular district can help administrators understand how to properly use evaluation as a tool. The purpose of evaluation systems can be either formative or summative in nature. Veir and Dagley (2002) define formative evaluation as follows:

> Formative evaluation, as used in the arena of teacher evaluation, is the process of analyzing the strengths and weaknesses of the educator. These evaluations provide opportunities for both the teacher and the administrator to reflect on the educator's performance, to obtain feedback, and to provide for the professional development of the educator.
>
> (p. 8)

At least 15 states provide formative statements of purpose. These statements of purpose include some or all of the following: "...professional growth, constructive assistance for teachers, improvement of instruction, improvement of performance, curriculum enhancement, identification of behaviors that contribute to student progress, and improvement of educational services" (Veir & Dagley, 2002, p. 7). Few states list summative purposes, such as evidence used to aid in teacher dismissal. Some states list both summative and formative purposes, but these statutes provide little guidance for implementation.

States and localities may also prescribe how the results of an evaluation are to be used. At least 18 states have laws that prescribe how the results of teacher evaluations are to be used. While the stated purpose of an evaluation system may be either formative or summative, "the stated use of the teacher evaluation system is invariably for summative purposes" (Veir & Dagley, 2002, p. 8). In a summative system, an administrator uses data collected from a teacher evaluation as evidence of the need for changes or improvements sought, including changes in employment status.

In some states, the stated purpose and use of teacher evaluations are in conflict. For example, a state statute may list the purpose of conducting teacher evaluations as formative, intended only to improve teaching practices. However, in the same state, evaluations may be used in making decisions regarding teachers' employment. Such a lack of consistency may make it difficult for educators to understand why they are being evaluated and what will happen with any information gathered in an evaluation.

Ensuring Legality in Evaluation

Despite the continued focus on teacher evaluation over the last few decades, no one system has emerged as the "right" way to evaluate teachers. However, through legislative efforts and court opinions, certain factors have been identified as legally necessary and/or desirable for evaluation systems. If evaluation systems are purely formative in both purpose and use, states and school districts are not confined by the strictures of state and federal law. However, if the evaluations are summative, particularly in use, and are used in making decisions regarding employee sanctions or employment status, the evaluation procedures must conform to due process requirements.

To comply with the requirements of state and federal law, an evaluation system must meet the following criteria:

1 **Adequate notice**: It must provide teachers with adequate notice of expectations regarding performance, consequences for noncompliance, and the teachers' rights.
2 **Hearing**: It must provide teachers subject to negative employment action (sanction, demotion, or termination) an opportunity to contest the disciplinary action.
3 **Avoidance of free-speech issues**: If the evaluation system requires assessments of teacher attitude or cooperation, it must account for potential free-speech issues.

Adequate Notice

To comply with the due process clause, an evaluation policy must be clear so that each teacher has adequate notice of what is required and prohibited. If the policy is unclear, a court may reverse a teacher sanction or termination on the grounds that the policy was vague or the criteria irrelevant. First, the criteria used in the evaluation must be rationally related to the state objectives. Second, the administrator should be able to demonstrate how each criterion is related to the job of teaching (Rossow & Tate, 2003). While the clarity of such objective criteria as whether class begins on time is easier to defend when challenged, such subjective criteria as whether the teacher explains something well are also necessary for a complete evaluation. Since subjective criteria require the evaluator to make discretionary judgments, it is particularly important that these criteria be presented clearly. Additionally, if an evaluation is used to inform a negative employment decision, the teacher must also be given adequate notice of all charges against him or her and the evidence that support the charges.

Hearings

Prior to dismissal or other negative employment action, school officials should provide the teacher with an opportunity to be heard. In fact, most states already have legislation governing the procedural protections afforded to state employees in such circumstances (Rossow & Tate, 2003). A hearing does not have to be elaborate. The hearing should take place before the teacher is sanctioned or dismissed and should allow the teacher to argue, either in writing or in person, against the proposed disciplinary action (*Cleveland Board of Education v. Loudermill*, 1985).

Avoidance of Free-Speech Issues

When evaluation criteria require assessments of attitude or cooperation, free-speech issues may be implicated (Rossow & Tate, 2003). A teacher's right to free speech is not extinguished simply because he or she has chosen to teach in a public school.[7] In *Pickering v. Board of Education* (1968), the U.S. Supreme Court ruled that teachers have a right to make known their views on matters of public concern. In fact, the Court determined that teachers may have a unique perspective that may lead to valuable contributions to the public debate. However, the Court determined that these protections do not necessarily extend to speech regarding coworkers and/or supervisors or speech that causes a disruption in the operation of the school (*Pickering v. Board of Education*, 1968). In *Mt. Healthy City School District v. Doyle* (1977) and *Connick v. Myers* (1983), the Court provided clarifications on when teacher speech is protected. The two opinions indicate that the more the speech has to do with matters of public concern, the more protected that speech will be. Alternatively, the more a teacher's speech interferes with his or her working relationships and/or the operation of the school, the less the speech is protected. Therefore, teacher evaluation criteria must be created with these issues in mind.

Emerging Legal Issues Associated with Teacher Evaluations, Including Value-Added Models

Ineffective teacher evaluation systems have made it difficult to identify poor and exceptional performance, to create appropriate interventions when necessary, and to terminate chronically underperforming teachers. The Race to the Top competitive grant program provided incentives for states to revise their teacher evaluation systems to better focus on teacher effectiveness (see Chapters 1 and 2). For most states applying for funding, this meant incorporating student test scores into teacher evaluations (Powell, 2013). While this evaluation technique is becoming increasingly popular, it may prove problematic for both practical and legal reasons. First, there is some concern about the statistical methodology used in calculating teacher impact based on student test scores (Darling-Hammond, 2009; Baker et al., 2010; Green, Baker, & Oluwole, 2012). Some districts have been exploring using test scores in VAMs, which attempt to isolate the impact of the teacher on a student's test score. However, research shows that these models are producing inconsistent results and focus excessively on math and reading scores to the exclusion of other subjects (Baker et al., 2010; Baker, Oluwole, & Green, 2013).

In practice, tying student test scores to teacher evaluations and employment decisions can "discourage teachers from wanting to work in schools with the neediest students, while the large, unpredictable variation in the results and their perceived unfairness can undermine teacher morale" (Baker et al., 2010, p. 4). It can also create a competitive rather than collaborative working environment, which can interfere with teachers working together to meet students' needs. Therefore, using student test scores in evaluating teachers may be professionally inappropriate. When student achievement data are used as part of an evaluation system, they should be used only as one component of a teacher's assessment (Educational Testing Service, 2005; Darling-Hammond, 2009).

As early as 1973, the courts began to consider whether using student test scores to evaluate teachers constituted a violation of teachers' rights to due process (Rossow & Tate, 2003). In *Scheelhaase v. Woodbury Central Community School District et al.* (1974), the court considered the validity of a teacher's non-renewal based solely on her students' achievement as evidenced by their performance on standardized tests. The teacher argued that because the use of student test scores was not supported by Iowa educational policy, her non-renewal constituted a violation of her right to substantive due process and that the test scores used as the basis of her non-renewal were not properly interpreted. While the trial court held in favor of the teacher, the court of appeals reversed.

The Court of Appeals for the Eighth Circuit held that a board of education and/or superintendent could rely on whatever expert opinions it wished to make its educational and employment decisions. In his concurring opinion, Circuit Judge Bright noted that "The Superintendent, in concluding on his experience that these test results reflected adversely on the teaching competence of Mrs. Scheelhaase, may have been erroneous but the conclusion was not an unreasoned one, and that is the test" (*Scheelhaase*, 1974, p. 245).

A decade later, the Supreme Court of Minnesota reached a similar conclusion in *Whaley v. Anoka-Hennepin Independent School District* (1982). In *Whaley*, a veteran teacher's termination was based in large part on a lack of student progress. The evidence of student progress included observations of students' speed, classroom observations, and progress on skills tests. The court ruled that there was sufficient evidence of poor student progress and upheld the teacher's termination. However, it is important to note that the teacher's impact on student progress was assessed using several different tools, only one of which was student performance on skills tests.

In the decades that followed, courts continued to support the use of student test scores as part of teachers' performance evaluations (*St. Louis Teachers Union, Local 420 v. St. Louis Board of Education*, 1987; *Indiana State Teachers Association v. Board of School Commissioners of Indianapolis*, 1998). In the last few years, the use of student performance indicators, particularly test scores, has become a larger part of teacher evaluations. As of 2012, at least 14 states require that at least 40% of a teacher's evaluation consist of student performance measures (Green et al., 2012). In fact, Colorado, Louisiana, and Tennessee have all enacted teacher evaluation systems that require 50% or more of a teacher's evaluation to be based on students' academic growth (Green et al., 2012).

As the number of states relying on student test scores to evaluate their teachers grows, particularly those systems based 50% or more on student achievement, litigation in this area is likely to increase as well. In fact, litigation concerning the use of student test scores in high-stakes decision making for teachers is already under way in several states. For example, on April 16, 2013, seven Florida teachers and three local teachers unions filed suit claiming that recent legislative changes to teacher tenure and evaluation procedures were arbitrary, irrational, and unfair as they applied to classroom teachers who did not teach classes tested by the state standardized test, in violation of their due process and equal protection rights (Blankenship, 2014). The act at issue required all classroom instructors to be evaluated annually using a value-added formula, using only state-approved assessments to measure student growth. However, statewide assessments for only reading and math for students in grades 4–10 were created in the initial program rollout, requiring schools to use student assessment scores in evaluations for teachers who did not teach those subjects or even those grades. In response to the litigation, the Florida legislature immediately went to work revising the system (Blankenship, 2014).

However, many more legal questions remain about the use of student test scores in summative teacher evaluations. Additional future litigation may rely on procedural and/or substantive due process, the equal protection clause of the Fourteenth Amendment, and Title VII of the Civil Rights Act of 1991 (Green et al., 2012). Due process challenges may be based on any of the following:

The instability of VAMs generally, with their high error rates; the non-random assignment of students, resulting in an uneven evaluation process; and a teacher's lack of control over the effort a student puts forth when taking the test, the student's support system at home, the student's physical and mental health on the day of the test, and so on. Additionally, the VAM could be challenged on equal protection or Title VII grounds if it has a racially disparate impact on teacher terminations (Baker et al., 2013).

Defamation in General

Defamation is a tort, or civil (as opposed to criminal), claim that is defined as "a false publication causing injury to a person's reputation, exposing the person to public hatred, contempt, ridicule, shame or disgrace, or affecting the person adversely in his or her trade or business" (Rossow & Tate, 2003, p. 95). Defamation can manifest itself through either written communications (called *libel*) or through oral communication (called *slander*). While defamation is generally a state law issue and varies from state to state, the essential elements of a defamation action are (1) the defendant made a false statement; (2) the false statement was defamatory; (3) the false statement was published; (4) the plaintiff was injured; and (5) the defendant acted with the required degree of fault (from negligent to malicious, depending on the circumstances) (*Sweitzer v. Outlet Communication, Inc.*, 1999).

Immunity for Government Employees

Public school teachers and administrators are entitled to some protections from individual liability for statements made on teacher evaluations if made within the course and scope of employment, even if they are later proven false. The term used to define this protection varies by state but is generally called *privilege* or *immunity*. The extent of the protection also is governed by state law and varies from state to state. Therefore, it is important for administrators to be familiar with their state and local laws to better avoid legal liability. For example, if a teacher files a defamation claim against an administrator, the administrator generally will be protected from personal liability if the administrator has followed proper procedure. However, if the administrator has somehow abused his or her position, then privilege or immunity will not protect the administrator from personal liability. The basic rules listed in this section will help administrators conduct evaluations without exposing themselves and their employers to legal liability.

Avoiding Defamation in Teacher Evaluations

Conducting performance evaluations is one of the necessary functions of an administrator or supervisor. However unpleasant, evaluations are imperative in assessing a teacher's strengths and weaknesses, professional development needs, and whether a teacher requires intervention or additional support from school administration. Because evaluations often require an administrator to report on a teacher's deficiencies and/or make critical remarks about the teacher, evaluations may open the door to claims of defamation. To avoid claims of defamation, administrators should follow three basic rules for conducting teacher evaluations (explained in more detail later in this section).

1   **Back it up with facts**: Use only facts (or opinions, in some cases) that are supported by evidence.
2   **Keep it in the circle**: Disclose the results of a teacher's evaluation to only "interested parties."
3   **Stay professional**: Evaluations should reflect the teacher's performance at work. Any thoughts regarding the teacher as an individual outside of the school are irrelevant and should not be included in an evaluation. The evaluator must be cognizant of his or her role in the evaluation process and avoid any abuse of power.

Backing Up Decisions with Facts

An essential element to a defamation claim is a false statement that is injurious to the reputation of another. Therefore, truth is always a great defense to a defamation claim. For example, in *Smith v. Des Moines Public Schools* (2001), Smith, a teacher, was fired for creating an unsafe work environment after a physical altercation with the school secretary over some school files. Smith was placed on administrative leave pending investigation and the secretary filed a complaint with the Des Moines Police Department, which led to Smith's arrest for assault. The parties signed a confidential settlement agreement and the charges against Smith were dropped (*Smith v. Des Moines Public Schools*, 2001, p. 943). However, Smith later filed suit against Des Moines Public Schools, claiming that its characterization of his behavior as creating an unsafe workplace was defamatory. The district argued, and the court agreed, that the district's allegedly defamatory remarks were substantially true because they bore the "sting or gist of the defamatory statement" (*Smith*, 2001, p. 945).

Lindemuth v. Jefferson County School District R-1 presents another example of the use of truth as a defense to a defamation suit. Lindemuth was fired from his job as an assistant basketball coach after his superior told several people that Lindemuth had a history of child molestation. In fact, 14 years earlier, Lindemuth pled "no contest" to a charge of sexual assault on a child. The court found in favor of the school district, holding that the statements were substantially true and that "[s]ubstantial truth is an absolute defense to a defamation claim" (*Lindemuth v. Jefferson County School District R-1*, 1988, p. 1058).

While the rules regarding truth and defamation are fairly straightforward, the courts' treatment of opinion has been less clear, particularly for school administrators. Traditionally, courts held that only statements of fact could serve as the basis for a defamation claim and that statements expressing opinions were protected. However, often the courts have found it difficult to distinguish between fact and opinion. Rossow and Tate (2003) note that "[i]n the context of a teacher evaluation, it would seem that an administrator's critical comments about a teacher often could be reasonably characterized as a statement of either fact or opinion" (p. 107). Therefore, it is important for administrators to be familiar with the relevant case law concerning both fact and opinion to protect against litigation.

In its 1990 opinion in *Milkovich v. Lorain Journal Co.*, the Supreme Court rejected the "wholesale defamation exemption for anything that might be labeled 'opinion'" (p. 18). The Court notes that under the common law, "defamatory communications were deemed actionable regardless of whether they were deemed to be statements of fact or opinion" (*Milkovich v. Lorain Journal Co.*, 1990, p. 13). However, to avoid stifling valuable public debate, the common law also provided a privilege of "fair comment" for statements regarding matters of public concern (pp. 13–14). Guided by both common law and case law, the Court states that providing a blanket protection for opinions in defamation suits "ignore[s] the fact that expressions of 'opinion' may often imply an assertion of objective fact" (p. 18). Therefore, the Court concludes that if "a statement of opinion relating to matters of public concern which does not contain a provable false factual connotation will receive full constitutional protection" (p. 20). In other words, if a statement of opinion can be proven true or false, it can be the subject of a defamation suit. However, if a statement of opinion cannot be proven false, then it constitutes free speech protected by the First Amendment.

The standards set forth in *Milkovich* apply specifically to cases involving media defendants. However, Rossow and Tate (2003) advise:

> School administrators should assume the standard does apply to them, and they should not rely on the kind of fact-opinion distinction courts have employed in the past. Administrators should further assume that any critical statements they make about teachers they are evaluating might be construed as fact statements that are fully actionable in a defamation suit.
>
> (p. 108)

Therefore, to protect themselves and their institutions, administrators should focus on facts, and opinions if necessary, that are supported by evidence. Including extraneous negative feedback on a teacher evaluation does little more than expose administrators and school districts to potential defamation suits.

Keeping It in the Circle

Immunity or privilege from liability in defamation cases often depends on whether the statement was made within the course and scope of the administrator's employment. That is determined by looking at when and where the statement was made and to whom it was disseminated. For example, in *Agins v. Darmstadter* (1989), a teacher brought a defamation suit against his superintendent for comments made to other district personnel during an investigation into the teacher's conduct. The court held that the superintendent could not be held liable for the comments because they were made in the course and scope of his official duties as superintendent.

However, this privilege or immunity is often restricted to communications between "interested" persons (Rossow & Tate, 2003). For example, in *Manguso v. Oceanside Unified School District* (1984), Manguso filed a libel suit against her former employer for statements made in a letter evaluating Manguso's performance that was placed in her college placement file at the University of Montana. The confidential master file of the teacher's employment history, including evaluations, was maintained by the university. The file was available to potential employers to assist them in making hiring decisions. The court concluded that the letter was protected by qualified privilege because it was "written by an educator, regarding qualifications of a particular teacher and directed to those prospective employers of that teacher" (*Manguso*, 1984, p. 580). However, had this information been disseminated to members of the general public who have no legitimate "interest" in the information, the administrator would not have received the same protections. Therefore, it is important that administrators be familiar with their particular state's law regarding who qualifies as an "interested person." To avoid personal and district liability, administrators must ensure that information regarding teacher evaluations and/or performance remains in the circle of "interested persons."

Staying Professional

The most common abuse of privilege committed by administrators in the evaluation process that results in defamation cases is malice (Rossow & Tate, 2003). States uniformly deny government employees privilege or immunity in defamation claims when the statement at issue was made with malice. While the definition varies from state to state, *malice* generally refers to situations in which the communicator has not acted in good faith and/or knows the statement(s) to be false. For example, in *Berlin v. Superintendent of Public Instruction* (1989), the Michigan court noted that government employees were entitled to immunity from tort liability only when they were acting in the course of their employment, performing discretionary acts, and "acting in good faith" (p. 766). Comparatively, in *Holland v. Kennedy* (1989), the Mississippi Supreme Court discusses malice in terms of "bad faith" and "statements made with knowledge of their falsity" (p. 987).

Therefore, to avoid personal liability, administrators *must* keep the evaluation process professional. Evaluations should focus only on a teacher's performance at work. Any personal thoughts that the administrator has regarding a teacher as an individual are irrelevant and should not be included in an evaluation. The evaluator always must be cognizant of his or her role in the evaluation process and avoid any abuse of power.

Procedures for Tackling Poor Performance

To ensure that legal challenges to negative employment actions are avoided, it is imperative that administrative procedures conform with the fundamental requirements of the due process clause of the Fourteenth Amendment to the U.S. Constitution. Rossow and Tate (2003) note that the due process clause requires the following:

> (1) using an evaluation instrument that is objective and that provides adequate notice to the teacher of the criteria that will be used and (2) an opportunity to remediate the deficiencies cited in the evaluation may be required by statutes, board policy, or collective agreement.
>
> (p. 37)

To fulfill these requirements, administrators should incorporate into their evaluation systems documentation and remediation. It is important to remember that since specific procedures and policies can vary from state to state and, at times, even district to district, administrators must be familiar with both their local regulations and constitutional requirements.

Documenting Teacher Conduct

In addition to the documentation that accompanies an observation, documentation memorializing notable events or behaviors throughout the school year should also be included in a teacher's file. Of course, a teacher's accolades and accomplishments should be included in his or her file for purposes of promotion, identification of teacher leaders, and compensation decisions. When a teacher performs poorly, this too must be included. An administrator can use this documentation to track a teacher's performance, to pinpoint problem areas and weaknesses, and to inform professional development needs. When poor performance turns into incompetence, the documented evidence of a teacher's attitude and behavior over a period of time will serve as the basis for any disciplinary or termination action.

Administrators should familiarize themselves with four kinds of memoranda to ensure full coverage.

Minor-incident memoranda

For more minor incidents that are worth note and ultimately should be considered in the teacher's evaluation but are not serious enough to warrant an immediate conference with the teacher, the administrator should prepare a short memorandum for the teacher's file. The format of the memorandum can vary based on the administrator's preference, as long as the format remains consistent. The memorandum should include the date, the name of the teacher, the name of the administrator, and details of the incident or behavior at issue. The administrator should include enough detail to refresh his or her memory regarding the incident at a later date (Frels & Horton, 2007).

Specific-incident memoranda

If there is a more serious incident, the principal should first hold a conference with the teacher to discuss what happened. Based on the outcome of that conference and any other investigation that is required, the administrator might want to consider drafting a specific-incident memorandum (Frels & Horton, 2007). This type of memorandum should summarize the complaint or incident as observed by the administrator or a third party, the teacher's response, the outcome of the conference, and any disciplinary or remedial actions that were taken. A copy of a specific-incident memorandum should be sent to the teacher and a copy should be placed in the teacher's file.

Summary memoranda

Summary memoranda should be used to document the results of a general conference with a teacher (Frels & Horton, 2007). These conferences can cover a number of topics, including but not limited to the results of classroom observations, any memoranda to file that have not already been discussed with the teacher, and any other general concerns. Summary memoranda should include the name of the teacher and the administrator, the date, facts pertaining to all issues and incidents discussed, and any directives to the teacher (Frels & Horton, 2007). A copy of the memorandum should be given to the teacher for review, with acknowledgment of receipt. If the teacher disagrees with any part of the memorandum, he or she should be encouraged to submit a written response that should be attached to the memorandum.

Visitation memoranda

Visitation memoranda are not used in all districts because much of this information is included in summary memoranda. In districts where visitation memoranda are used, the administrator can use this instrument to summarize a classroom visit or observation along with any suggestions for improvement. The contents should be reviewed with the teacher in a post-observation conference.

Developing and Managing a Plan of Improvement

When an administrator identifies a deficiency in a teacher's performance, state law often requires that the teacher be given a reasonable amount of time to improve (see Chapter 6). An administrator should provide the teacher with a plan for improvement that includes specific recommendations on what areas need work for the teacher to reach the expected level of competence and information regarding the means by which the teacher can obtain assistance and/or training (Rossow & Tate, 2003). The remediation plan should also establish a reasonable time period for improvement. The title of such a plan may vary from district to district; it may be called a *remediation plan*, a *plan of improvement*, a *personal development plan*, or something similar.

A remediation or improvement plan should address the following questions:

1   What behavior or conduct is expected of the teacher?
2   What precisely is unacceptable about the teacher's performance?
3   How is the teacher expected to change his or her performance? What is the teacher expected to do in the future?
4   What resources are available to the teacher to help them improve his or her performance (e.g., workshops, counseling, mentoring, and retraining, written technical assistance) (McGrath, 2006)?
5   How much time does the teacher have in which to make the listed improvements?
6   How are the teacher's improvements to be identified and measured?
7   What are the consequences if the teacher fails to improve his or her performance?

Note that every school district will have its own documentation for teacher evaluation and improvement. It is important that an administrator be familiar with all of the documents and procedures that his or her district uses in the evaluation process (see Chapter 5).

Moving Toward Termination

In spite of an administrator's best efforts, some teachers' performance will not improve under a remediation plan and termination will be necessary (see Chapter 9). At this point, the focus of the evaluation process becomes completely summative. Before moving forward with termination, an administrator must answer the following questions:

1   **What are the grounds for termination?** The grounds for termination are laid out in the state statute and may vary a bit. However, generally grounds for termination include incompetency, immorality, insubordination, willful neglect of duties, violation of state law or school board policy, and reduction in staff.

2   **Is termination a proportional and progressive sanction for the teacher's conduct?** Termination should not be the first sanction to which an administrator turns. Sanctions should increase as necessary. Generally, state or district policy will establish what steps must be taken before a teacher can be terminated. For example, if a teacher is not displaying proper classroom management, a written warning should be the first step, followed by an in-person conference and a remediation plan. If, after those steps, the teacher has not made the requisite improvement, then termination may be appropriate. A documented proportional and progressive approach will help to fulfill the requirements of substantive and procedural due process (Dayton, 2012).

3   **Is there enough documented evidence to withstand a challenge in court?** Of course, gathering documented evidence that will stand up in court is a process that takes time. To ensure that there is always sufficient evidence to terminate a teacher if that becomes necessary, administrators should make documentation a habit. Whenever a teacher does something that does not conform to performance expectations, it should be documented. After some time, documentation should become second nature.

If these three questions can be answered satisfactorily, then an administrator should feel comfortable proceeding with termination. While never pleasant, terminating an incompetent teacher will ultimately benefit the health of the entire school, particularly the students.

Of course, an administrator should include the central office and the school district's attorney in the termination process. Legal counsels are most effective when they are brought into a case early, before significant errors have been made. An attorney can give guidance about the strength of a case and can help the administrator to comply with due process requirements, state laws, and deadlines (Manning, 1988).

In summary, administrators have a legal duty to evaluate their teachers, identify poor performance, and provide underperforming teachers with resources for remediation. Additionally, as instructional leaders, administrators have a moral duty to help the teachers in their schools to perform at the highest level. They must do whatever it takes to ensure that students are receiving appropriate instruction. This chapter discusses the legal issues and challenges that can arise when supervising underperforming and incompetent teachers. To avoid the courtroom, administrators *must* have a working knowledge of their district's evaluation system and laws governing teacher sanctions and terminations. Proper use of a district's evaluation system will help an administrator to identify underperforming and incompetent teachers, appropriately document issues regarding teacher conduct, plan and execute a remediation plan and, when necessary, terminate incompetent teachers.

An administrator should always remain optimistic when working with an underperforming teacher. When an underperforming teacher is able to improve his or her performance and become a successful educator, everybody wins. Unfortunately, the reality is that not every teacher will be able or willing to improve under a remediation plan. Therefore, an administrator must make the evaluation system procedures a part of the everyday routine. If an administrator consistently sticks to the evaluation system and is cognizant of potential legal issues, he or she can focus more on the classroom and less on the courtroom. Finally, the school leader is encouraged to go beyond the scope of this chapter through extended reading, discussing the parameters of work within his or her school system and, if necessary, to seek the counsel of central office administration and legal counsel.

Notes

1 This chapter was written by Ann Elizabeth Blankenship, J.D., Ph.D. Dr. Blankenship is an Assistant Professor of Educational Law and Leadership at the University of Southern Mississippi, the associate editor-in-chief of the *Education Law and Policy Review*, and a former civil litigation attorney. She received her Ph.D. in educational administration and policy from the University of Georgia and her J.D. from the University of Tennessee College of Law. Her research focuses on teacher personnel and social justice issues in education.

2 All information in this document is intended solely for general educational purposes. This information is not intended as legal advice. Legal advice can be obtained only from a qualified attorney in your state, based on the unique circumstances of your case.

3 Nearly all states have a provision in their state constitution guaranteeing the same rights to due process. Therefore, those rights are both state and federal.

4 Because public schools are operated by the government, their employees are considered state agents and their actions can be considered government actions.

5 Note that these are just some examples of common grounds for termination. Each state has different grounds that may or may not include these grounds and more.

6 A teacher has a property right to employment for the period that he or she has a contract for employment. If a non-tenured teacher's employment is terminated mid-contract, he or she is entitled to due process of law. If, however, a non-tenured teacher's contract is simply not renewed, the non-tenured teacher is not entitled to due process.

7 Note that private school teachers are not employed by the state and so they are not agents of the state or controlled by agents of the state. Therefore, the same constitutional protections do not apply to private school teachers.

References

Agins v. Darmstadter, 153 A.D.2d 600 (N.Y. App. Div. 1989).

Baker, B. D., Oluwole, J. O., & Green, P. C., III (2013). The legal consequences of mandating high stakes decisions based on low quality information: Teacher evaluation in the Race-to-the-Top era. *Education Policy Analysis Archives, 21*(5), 1–71. doi: 10.14507/epaa.v21n5.2013

Baker, E. L, Barton, P. E., Darling-Hammond, L. D., Haertel, E., Ladd, H. F, Linn, R. L., et al. (2010). *Problems with the use of student test scores to evaluate teachers* [Policy briefing paper #278]. Washington, D.C.: Economic Policy Institute. Retrieved from http://s2.epi.org/files/page/-/pdf/bp278.pdf

Berlin v. Superintendent of Pub. Instruction, 448 N.W.2d 764 (Mich. Ct. App. 1989).

Blankenship, A. E. (2014). Teacher tenure: The times they are a changin'. *Education Law and Policy Review, 1*, 193–227. Retrieved from http://educationlawconsortium.org/yahoo_site_admin/assets/docs/ELPR_Vol_1.114110723.pdf

Board of Regents of State Coll. v. Roth, 408 U.S. 564 (1972).

Bridges, E. M. (1992). *The incompetent teacher: Managerial responses*. Washington, D.C.: Falmer Press.

Cleveland Bd. of Educ. v. Loudermill, 470 U.S. 532 (1985).

Cohen, E., & Walsh, K. (2010). Invisible ink in teacher contracts. *Education Next, 10,* 18–23. Retrieved from http://educationnext.org/invisible-ink-in-teacher-contracts

Connick v. Myers, 461 U.S. 138 (1983).

Darling-Hammond, L. (2000). Teacher quality and student achievement: A review of state policy evidence. *Educational Policy Analysis Archives, 8*(1), 1–44. doi: 10.14507/epaa.v8n1.2000

Darling-Hammond, L. (2009). Recognizing and enhancing teacher effectiveness. *International Journal of Educational and Psychological Assessment, 3,* 1–24. Retrieved from http://www.warreninstitute3.org/images/download/RT_031011/AR/L_Darling Hammond_Recognizing__Enhancing_Teacher_Effectiveness.pdf

Dayton, J. (2012). *Education law: Principles, policies, and practice.* Bangor, ME: Wisdom Builders Press.

Education Commission of the States. (2007). *Teacher tenure/continuing contract laws: Updated for 2007* [Data file]. Retrieved from http://www.ecs.org/clearinghouse/75/64/7564.pdf

Educational Testing Service. (2005). *Using student progress to evaluate teachers: A primer on value added models.* Princeton, NJ: Henry Braun. Retrieved from http://www.ets.org/Media/Research/pdf/PICVAM.pdf

Frels, K., & Horton, J. L. (2007). *A documentation system for teacher improvement or termination* (6th ed.). Dayton, OH: Education Law Association.

Fuhr, D. (1990). Supervising the marginal teacher. *Here's How: National Association of Elementary School Principals, 9*(2), 2–6. Retrieved from http://files.eric.ed.gov/fulltext/ED324825.pdf

Green, P. C. III, Baker, B. D., & Oluwole, J. (2012). The legal and policy implications of value-added teacher assessment policies. *Brigham Young University Education and Law Journal, 2012*(1/2), 1–29. Retrieved from http://digitalcommons.law.byu.edu/elj/vol2012/iss1/2

Hanushek, E. A. (1992). The trade-off between child quantity and quality. *Journal of Political Economy, 100*(1), 84–117. doi: 10.1086/261808

Hanushek, E. A., & Rivkin, S. G. (2006). Teacher quality. In E. A. Hanushek & F. Welch (Eds.), *Handbook of the economics of education* (Vol. 2, pp. 2–24). Amsterdam: North-Holland.

Holland v. Kennedy, 548 So.2d 982 (Miss. 1989).

Indiana State Teachers Ass'n v. Bd. of Sch. Comm'rs of Indianapolis, 693 N.E. 2d 972 (Ind. 1998).

Lawrence, C. E., Vachon, M. K., Leake, D. O., & Leake, B. H. (2005). *The marginal teacher: A step-by-step guide to fair procedures for identification and dismissal* (3rd ed.). Thousand Oaks, CA: Corwin.

Lindemuth v. Jefferson Cnty. Sch. Dist. R-1, 765 P.2d 1057 (Colo. Ct. App. 1988).

Manguso v. Oceanside Unified Sch. Dist., 153 Cal. App. 3d 574 (Cal. Ct. App. 1984).

Manning, R. C. (1988). *The teacher evaluation handbook: Step-by-step techniques and forms for improving instruction.* Englewood Cliffs, NJ: Prentice Hall.

McGrath, M. J. (2006). Dealing positively with nonproductive teachers. In J. H. Stronge (Ed.). *Evaluating teaching: A guide to current thinking and best practices* (2nd ed., pp. 253–267). Thousand Oaks, CA: Corwin.

Milkovich v. Lorain Journal Co., 497 U.S. 1 (1990).

Mt. Healthy City Sch. Dist. v. Doyle, 429 U.S. 274 (1977).

Painter, S. (2000). Principals' perceptions of barriers to teacher dismissal. *Journal of Personnel Evaluation in Education, 14*(3), 253. doi: 10.1023/A:1008144215978

Perez v. Comm'n on Prof'l Competence, 149 Cal.App.3d 1167 (Cal. Dist. Ct. App., 1983).

Pickering v. Bd. of Educ., 391 U.S. 563 (1968).

Powell, E. (2013). The quest for teacher quality: Early lessons from Race to the Top and state legislative efforts regarding teacher evaluation. *DePaul Law Review, 62*, 1061–1093. Retrieved from http://via.library.depaul.edu/law-review/vol62/iss4/7

Rossow, L. F., & Tate, J. O. (2003). *The law of teacher evaluation* (2nd ed.). Dayton, OH: Education Law Association.

Scheelhaase v. Woodbury Cent. Cmty. Sch. Dist. et al., 488 F.2d 237 (8th Cir. 1973), *cert. denied*, 417 U.S. 969 (1974).

Smith v. Des Moines Pub. Sch., 259 F. 3d 942 (8th Cir. 2001).

St. Louis Teachers Union, Local 420 v. St. Louis Bd. of Educ., 652 F. Supp. 425 (E.D. Mo. 1987).

Sweitzer v. Outlet Commc'n, Inc., 726 N.E.2d 1084 (Ct. App. Ohio 1999).

Tigges, J. H. (1965). What constitutes "incompetency" or "inefficiency" as a ground for dismissal or demotion of public school teacher. *American Law Reports 3d, 4*, 1090–1140.

Tucker, P. D. (1997). Lake Wobegon: Where all teachers are competent (or, have we come to terms with the problem of incompetent teachers?). *Journal of Personnel Evaluation in Education, 11*(2), 103. doi: 10.1023/A:1007962302463

Veir, C. A., & Dagley, D. L. (2002). Legal issues in teacher evaluation legislation: A study of state statutory provisions. *Brigham Young University Education and Law Journal, 2002*(1), 1–16. Retrieved from http://digitalcommons.law.byu.edu/elj/vol2002/iss1/2

Weisberg, D., Sexton, S., Mulhern, J., & Kelling, D. (2009). *The widget effect: Our national failure to acknowledge and act on differences in teacher effectiveness* (2nd ed.). Brooklyn, NY: The New Teacher Project. Retrieved from http://tntp.org/assets/documents/TheWidgetEffect_2nd_ed.pdf

Whaley v. Anoka-Hennepin Indep. Sch. Dist., 325 N.W.2d 128 (Minn. 1982).

The Consequences of Doing Nothing and Making Tough Decisions When All Else Fails

9

As the leader, you must make the decision about the direction to follow with an underperforming teacher. This is the type of decision that cannot be delegated. In other words, it is time to (1) extend a modified plan of improvement for the following year, (2) sign off that the teacher on the plan of improvement has made enough progress to come off the plan, or (3) move toward non-renewal or possibly dismissal.

On a personal level, having to let a teacher know that he or she has reached the end of the road and the next step leads to the exit door is gut wrenching. The underperforming teacher's career will more than likely not easily recover from having a non-renewal on the record. Tensions will mount if the underperforming teacher is a really nice person, is well liked by faculty, or lives in the community.

At the end of the day, an underperforming teacher is doing damage to students, the instructional program of the school and, perhaps, the community. Parents and community members know who the underperforming teachers are. They are the parents who call the school, meet with leaders, and make formal requests for their children to be moved out of or not assigned to the teacher's classroom.

Doing Nothing—Ethical, Moral, Legal, and Financial Consequences

Accountability harkens and leaders must serve their schools by acting on teachers whose performance prevents students from learning. There is no room for the underperforming teacher whose skills still do not meet expectations as set forth in a formal plan of improvement (see Chapter 6). Many ethical, moral, financial, and legal issues surround working with underperforming teachers whose performance does not improve through the supports offered to them. There are also consequences—intended and unintended—that surround the work with underperforming teachers. These consequences ratchet up the closer an underperforming teacher moves toward possible non-renewal or recommendation for termination.

Ethical and Moral Issues

Moral outrage should exist among our citizens, including school leaders, teachers, parents, community and business members, and students themselves, if underperforming teachers who qualify as marginal or worse are allowed to continue teaching. This outrage will echo louder for leaders who tolerate teachers who are on formal plans of improvement when the results land in a category in which "little to no improvement" or "unsatisfactory" would be marked on a summative evaluation (see Chapter 2).

Morally and ethically, leaders who put a teacher on a plan of improvement have acted with due diligence because remediation is "simply the right thing to do" (Nolan & Hoover, 2011, p. 300). Leaders are doing the right thing by trying "to eliminate mediocre or poor teaching" through consistent supports offered as part of the plan of improvement (Jackson, 2008, p. 9). If, over an appropriate period of support, the underperforming teacher shows little improvement, his or her potential for competent independence as an effective instructor is low.

The leader who lets the underperforming teacher stay compromises the ethic of due diligence. No response to act on the best interest of students is an ethical and a moral issue (Kaye, 2004; Maulding & Joachim, 2000). Kaye (2004) shares, "The need to understand marginal teaching is the need to understand what is good or not good for children. This need was and remains a moral obligation" (p. 235).

An ethical issue that leaders face is whether to give blatantly underperforming teachers the latitude to resign. On a moral level, resignation wipes clean the slate and essentially reduces the leader de facto to engaging in the game of "pass the trash" to another system. Is it fair to other school systems to hire blindly a teacher who has been deemed unsatisfactory elsewhere but has been afforded the opportunity to resign versus not being renewed or being terminated?

Moreover, a non-renewed teacher will more than likely want to list the principal as a reference, expecting a glowing report. Having to provide a reference could place the principal in a moral dilemma. Fullan (2002) underscores that "moral purpose is social responsibility to others and the environment," and leaders must "act with the intention of making a positive difference in their own schools as well as improving the environment in other district schools (p. 17). Although it might feel good and remove some of the sting that the principal experiences, passing off an underperforming teacher from one system to another does not improve conditions for students or promote better school systems.

Legal and Financial Issues

The hands of school systems are often tied by union entanglements and lengthy processes that are fatiguing to both the system and the school leader. The legal issues surrounding non-renewal and dismissal are examined in Chapter 8. It is not uncommon for school leaders to avoid the process of non-renewal or dismissal because "they view the dismissal process as overly time consuming and cumbersome, and the outcomes for those who do invest the time in the process is uncertain" (Weisberg, Sexton, Mulhern, & Keeling, 2009, p. 17).

Not confronting marginal teachers comes at a high cost: Tucker (1997) tells us, "The learning inequity created by incompetent teachers for millions of children each year cannot be ignored" (p. 11). The following figures associated with dismissal have been reported in the media:

- Eltman (2008) reports in New York: "[T]he cost to fire one incompetent tenured teacher is about $250,000" from the pockets of taxpayers (para. 15).
- Harris (2014) reports in the Los Angeles Unified School District: "[T]he average cost of dismissing an ineffective teacher, which involves as many as 17 administrative steps, is $250,000 to $450,000, with many cases costing districts more" (para. 13).

The Center for Union Facts (n.d.) asks, rhetorically:

> So why don't districts try to terminate more of their poor performers? The sad answer is that their chance of prevailing is vanishingly small. Teachers unions have ensured that even with a victory, the process is prohibitively expensive and time consuming.
>
> (para. 15)

The financial and emotional strain for school leaders makes non-renewal or dismissal less than appealing. Many school leaders are "reluctant to move for dismissal because they have heard horror stories of dismissal attempts that were extremely costly and were eventually overturned by the courts because of some minor procedural error" (Nolan & Hoover, 2011, p. 316).

Is it time to stay or leave? To answer this question, the school leader focuses on data and evidence by pulling the pieces together so that an informed decision can be made and then communicated with authority to an underperforming teacher.

Artifacts and Evidence—Pulling the Pieces Together

The administrator has the task of judging the underperforming teacher's performance against identified markers of improvement. Throughout the formal plan of improvement, the principal has been engaged in the process of having difficult conversations, observing in the teacher's classroom, examining other types of data—essentially collecting artifacts and evidence that support performance. Although the dismissal of a tenured teacher is rare (Bridges, 1990), the paper trail needed to move toward non-renewal or dismissal must be substantial and detailed, and these tasks take time and energy. Lawrence, Vachon, Leake, and Leake (2005) state, "The documentation must show that an intensive assistance plan was established and implemented for the teacher using school and district resources and that the teacher was given a reasonable length of time to improve performance" (p. 74). Moreover, "documentation …must be 'airtight,' [and] you must prove that the teacher failed to improve teaching performance, thereby hindering student achievement and learning opportunities in the classroom" (Lawrence et al., 2005, p. 78).

Documentation and Data Sources

Data are concrete and observable and, for the underperforming teacher, principals assemble the artifacts and evidence they have. Principals analyze artifacts and evidence to help assess the progress of a teacher on a formal plan of improvement (see Chapter 6).

Data and artifacts are derived from

1   **Classroom observations**: notes from classroom observations and forms from required or additional observations.
2   **Annual goals** and reports of progress toward meeting goals.
3   **Pre- and post-observation conferences**: artifacts that drove the discussion in the pre- and post-observation conferences; written commentaries related to the performance standards and their elements.
4   **Additional artifact sources**: such as student artifacts viewed during classroom observations, as received from the teacher, as examined to guide pre-observation conferences, the subsequent classroom observation(s), and conversations in the post-observation conference(s).
5   **Rating patterns**: in informal and formal classroom observations including, for example, *exemplary*, *proficient*, *emerging*, and *unsatisfactory*.
6   **Plans of improvement**: evidence related to professional development on areas marked as in need of improvement.
7   **Duties and responsibilities**: attendance patterns, participation in team and grade-level meetings.
8   **Correspondence**: notes and memos shared with the teacher.
9   **Results of survey data**: student and parent ratings of teachers.
10 **Student achievement data**.

Analysis of Evidence—Looking for Patterns

Here are some ideas to help principals frame data and its analysis for reflection while assessing overall teacher performance.

- **Hold subjectivities:** No matter how hard we try, subjectivity can creep into the ways we interpret results across all pieces of data. Data are evidence; interpretation of evidence needs to be objective, free of bias, whether positive or negative.

- **Create a chain of evidence:** Assemble data and look at the totality of the teacher's performance. The chain of evidence helps to increase objectivity and decrease subjectivity.
- **Review key documents:** Key documents to support the thinking and the writing of the required narrative on the annual teacher evaluation form are replete with the language of a standards-based and performance-based learning environment.
- **Golden rule**: To increase objectivity and to decrease subjectivity, criteria must be applied to *only one teacher at a time*.
- **It's all about totality:** All aspects of the teacher's performance need to be reflected in the final rating.

With these principles in mind and with data, the principal can make an assessment of progress toward improvement. The following vignette along with supporting documentation illustrates two things: (1) how to begin framing a decision that is (2) based on data found within the artifacts and evidence. A sampling of artifacts is also presented in the case of the fictional Mr. Robert Jansky. The artifacts include the following:

- Artifact 1: Meet Mr. Jansky—Timeline Leading to the Initiation of a Plan of Improvement
- Artifact 2: August 19, 2014 Memo—Students Unsupervised in the Halls
- Artifact 3: August 26, 2014 Memo—Students Seeking Section Transfers
- Artifact 4: October 3, 2014—Plan of Improvement
- Artifact 5: October 6, 2014—Memo Summarizing Initial Meeting with Mr. Jansky.

Artifact 1: Meet Mr. Jansky

Mr. Robert Jansky is a fifth-year teacher of mathematics in his first year at Stenson Williams High School, and Mr. Forbes has been the principal at Stenson for 11 years. On September 18, 2014, Mr. Jack Forbes observed Mr. Jansky's Algebra I class for 40 minutes. Mr. Forbes observed: (1) students acting out throughout the lesson; (2) Mr. Jansky sitting at his desk for 10 minutes as students were doing "drills," ignoring students who had their hands raised; (3) three subject-matter errors made by Mr. Jansky, who lost his temper when five students tried to seek clarification about the errors; (4) a sarcastic remark made by Mr. Jansky when a student asked for additional help ("Maybe your mommy can hire a tutor for you" followed by "I can tell you aren't the sharpest tool in the shed"); and (5) students preparing for the class to end—packing their bags, putting on coats, and talking—9 minutes before the bell.

Established rituals and routines were absent as students entered the classroom: (1) Students sat idly talking before the bell. (2) When the bell rang, Mr. Jansky took 5 minutes to settle students down; for students to take out their materials for the day; and for Mr. Jansky to turn on the computer. Two students were asked to sit in the hallway [Artifact 2: August 19, 2014 Memo—Students Unsupervised in the Halls].

The room was messy: trash on the floor, books, and papers cluttering Mr. Jansky's desk, with one stack falling to the floor when he was looking for a book of problems.

During the post-observation conference, Mr. Jansky indicated students were "troubled" and three students were in the process of transferring sections.

Three concerns were discussed at length:

1   Routines and rituals need to be revisited.
2   Instructional strategies that go beyond having students "work out the answer to the problem" need to be used.
3   Lesson plans were not available for the current week or the week prior to the classroom observation.

After the meeting, Mr. Forbes visited with the freshman counselor and was told that Mr. Jansky's class started with 24 students and had 19 now with 3 students requesting transfers [Artifact 3: August 26, 2014 Memo—Students Seeking Section Transfers].

Mr. Forbes asked assistant principal Dr. Maria Sanchez, who oversees the Mathematics Department, to conduct an informal classroom observation in a few days, visiting a different class period.

On September 23, 2014, Dr. Sanchez noted in her post-observation discussion two additional concerns: (1) The content standards were not being taught following the district curriculum, pacing guide, and best practices that the district had adopted. (2) Mr. Jansky became defensive when students asked for clarification or additional explanations, and he sent two students to the hallway, an issue that had been addressed on August 19, 2014.

On September 25, 2014, Mr. Forbes started receiving phone calls from parents who were concerned because (1) their children were becoming confused, (2) student misbehavior was making it difficult for students to learn, and (3) Mr. Jansky refused to meet before or after with students who asked for extra help.

During an extended conversation between Mr. Forbes and Mr. Jansky on September 29, 2014, it became evident that Mr. Jansky needed extra support offered through a formalized plan of improvement.

On October 3, 2014, Mr. Jansky was put on a formal plan of improvement (Artifact 4—Plan of Improvement; and Artifact 5—October 6, 2014 Memo Summarizing Initial Meeting with Mr. Jansky).

Artifact 2: August 19, 2014 Memo— Students Unsupervised in the Halls

From: Dr. Lucille Sanchez, Assistant Principal
To: Robert Jansky
Subject: Classroom Supervision—Students in the Hallway
Date: August 19, 2014

This memo is a follow-up to our conversation on Monday, August 18, 2014, and to outline the expectations about not "throwing students out of class" because they are rowdy, do not have a pencil, or you believe they are asking questions to slow down your lecture.

You cannot remove students from the classroom to sit in the hallways for any length of time.

Mr. Forbes shared during the first faculty meeting that teachers cannot put students out of classrooms unsupervised. In our conversation, you did agree that you remembered Mr. Forbes addressing this expectation; however, you admitted that you do not feel this is a reasonable procedure. I spoke to you a week ago about students being disruptive in your class and reminded you that (1) students must at all times be supervised and (2) if there is a serious problem, let the office know through the bell system. You verbally agreed that these notions were reasonable.

It is the expectation that students will not be unsupervised. I appreciate your assurance on this matter and hope that you will seek additional assistance with classroom management techniques. Mr. Cartwright and Ms. Kennedy have agreed to share some tips and cues with you.

Please sign acknowledging receipt of this memo and return by noon, Friday, August 22, 2014.

_____

(Signature)   (Date)

Artifact 3: August 26, 2014 Memo—
Students Seeking Section Transfers

Date: August 26, 2014
From: Dr. Lucille Sanchez, Assistant Principal
To: Robert Jansky
Subject: Students Seeking Section Transfer

Yesterday, I met with Mr. Tadd Herrington, Counselor and Head of Student Scheduling, to ensure that our courses were leveled. While looking at course and section enrollments, it was brought to my attention that your Algebra I courses have the fewest number of students enrolled, primarily because students or their parents are requesting transfers to other sections taught by different teachers.

The Algebra I classes you teach have fewer students than any other Algebra I sections. This is an inequity that is not fair to our colleagues and, moreover, puts students in classes that have 25 or more students whereas your sections have about 14 students.

At this juncture, we need to meet to discuss the reasons that students are asking for transfers from your courses. We can meet tomorrow, August 27. I'll come to your room as it is open during this hour.

Artifact 4: October 3, 2014—Plan of Improvement

Teacher: Mr. Robert Jansky   Date: October 3, 2014

Accompanying Meeting Summary Memo Attached

Section I: Areas of Concern

Concern Area 1: **Classroom Rituals and Routines**

Description of Current Weakness: Students are not aware of classroom procedures at the beginning of class. Students chatter when Mr. Jansky is speaking and while other students answer questions. Students are not aware of expectations for behavior (e.g., how to answer a question posed) as evidenced by the blurting of responses.

Related Artifact and Evidence: classroom observation notes; memo related to putting students out of class, unsupervised in the hallway.

Concern Area 2: **Alignment of Instruction to District Guidelines**

Description of Current Weakness: The content of Algebra I is not aligned to district guidelines and pacing guidelines.

Related Artifact and Evidence: lesson plans, classroom observations

Section II: Objectives and Goals for Improvement

Area 1 Objectives and Goals for Improvement:

Develop classroom rituals and routines (e.g., entering the classroom) and enforce them (e.g., appropriate response when students misbehave) without throwing students out of class.

Area 2 Objectives and Goals for Improvement:

Consult the district curriculum and pacing guides and (1) follow the scope and sequence of the content; (2) align instructional strategies to the ones offered in the pacing guide; (3) submit lesson plans for the department head to review; (4) align assessments to match content goals.

Section III: Strategies to Meet Improvement

Area 1 Strategies to Meet Improvement:

1. Meet with the dean of students to discuss appropriate rituals and routines.
2. Identify rituals and routines that you will communicate to students via a one-page handout.
3. Set appropriate consequences for students who do not meet expectations.
4. Submit to Dr. Sanchez, the dean of students, and me the handout for review before giving to students.
5. Spend 20 minutes explaining the routines and rituals in each class.

Area 2 Strategies to Meet Improvement:

1. Develop lesson plans that align with content and objectives.
2. Arrange class session according to the standards of practice.

Section IV: Support and Resources

Area 1 Support and Resources:

Provided by: dean of students; assistant principal

Area 2 Support and Resources:

Provided by: department chair; assistant principal; math coach

Section V: Timelines to Meet Areas of Concern

Area 1 Timeline to Meet Areas of Concern: September 23, 2014–January 15, 2015

Area 2 Timeline to Meet Areas of Concern: September 23, 2014–January 15, 2015

Section VI: Monitoring the Plan			
Area of Concern	Supports and Resources	Provided by/ Date	Progress Toward Improvement
Area 1	Dean of students; assistant principal	*[To be completed]*	*[To be completed]*
Area 2	Department chair; assistant principal; math coach	*[To be completed]*	*[To be completed]*

This plan spans from October 3, 2014 to January 2015. Written and oral feedback will be given formally on October 15, November 17, and December 12, 2014, and January 15, 2015.

Principal's Signature _____ Date _____

Teacher's Signature _____ Date _____

Section VII: Recommendation Based on Outcome of Formalized Plan of Improvement

☐ Sufficient improvement has been achieved: The teacher is no longer on a formalized plan of improvement.

☐ Some improvement has been achieved, but more improvement is needed. The teacher remains on a formalized plan of improvement and modifications to the formalized plan of improvement have been made.

☐ Little or no improvement has been achieved. The teacher is recommended for non-renewal, dismissal, or termination.

Artifact 5: October 6, 2014—Memo Summarizing Initial Meeting with Mr. Jansky

Date: October 6, 2014
To: Mr. Robert Jansky
From: Mr. Jack Forbes
Subject: Plan of Improvement Meeting Summary

You were placed on a plan of improvement because of concerns primarily with (1) the absence of routines and rituals; (2) failure of instruction and content of Algebra I to follow district pacing guides, including performance standards (state) and failure of assessments to align with standards; and (3) issues related to communicating with students (specifically, sarcasm).

Routines and Rituals
Several areas of concern were noted related to an absence of clearly defined and consistently enforced expectations for student behavior. The lack of classroom routines and rituals has fostered a learning environment where (1) students are being sent unattended into the hallways for misbehavior; (2) students blurt out answers and talk over you and other students trying to answer or ask questions; and (3) sarcasm marks communication patterns with students (e.g., "Ask your mommy to hire a tutor"; "Ask someone who cares"; "Do you think I care about what happens when you are trying to do this on your own?"). Sarcasm will never be accepted, and this behavior and pattern of communication must cease immediately. Related to the learning environment and the absence of classroom rituals and routines, an inordinate number of parent complaints have surfaced, and numerous students are seeking a transfer out of your classes (Algebra I).

Instruction and Course Content
Lesson plans based on the performance standards using research-based strategies for instruction and assessing student learning must align to the system pacing guides for Algebra I. Specifically, lesson plans were not

submitted in a timely manner that reflects the standards found in the pacing guides. Classroom instruction did not follow your lesson plans or adhere to the pacing guide for Algebra I. The plan of improvement is to support you to plan and to assess instruction and to create a more positive learning environment. The following are the areas on your plan of improvement and the concerns shared during our meeting.

1   **Lesson plans must be submitted every Monday morning to your department chair. Lesson plans must follow the district pacing guide.** Because you have not been submitting your lesson plans in a timely manner, nor were you connecting them to the state standards for Algebra I, this area becomes a part of your plan of improvement. All teaching and learning will reflect and be built around the system's guides.

    The expectation is that you must follow the scope and sequence of the district content and pacing guide that is aligned to the state standards for Algebra I.

2   **Classroom instruction must clearly adhere to the weekly lesson plans to be submitted on time.** You must follow the lesson plans submitted to ensure that you are following the pacing guide and implementing the state standards for Algebra I. In the past, your lesson plans were submitted to the department chair but not implemented in the classroom. Also, lesson plans submitted did not always follow the state standards or keep pace with the Algebra I guide. The expectation is that planning and teaching must be directly linked to the state standards.

    Dr. Sanchez and I noted in our classroom observations that students appeared confused, and we based this overall assessment on the questions they were asking and the responses you were giving. The sarcasm associated with your responses (addressed earlier in the summary) did not help put students at ease or better their understanding of concepts.

3 **Assessment of student work must align to the state standards found in the Algebra I content guide.**

In our meeting, you disclosed that you have not administered the pre-test assessment; therefore, you have no information related to student performance to guide the development of your teaching (re-teaching concepts, offering additional support for struggling students, or enrichment for students who have mastered content); moreover, assessment data can support differentiating instruction and learning activities and provide opportunities for enrichment. We are in the ninth week of school, four grades are in the record book, and no pre-test scores have been posted.

4 **Clear rituals and routines must be developed and implemented with clear consequences.** Routines for the beginning and the ending of the period must be established; consequences for students not following classroom rituals and routines must be consistently applied.

Sarcasm, belittling students, and sending students who misbehave into the hallway will not be tolerated. It is expected that you will be respectful of students and that includes answering their questions.

The purpose of this letter is to summarize our meeting during which we discussed deficiencies in your performance. My expectation continues that you will meet all requirements of your plan of improvement.

Signature _____ Date _____

Your signature acknowledges receipt of this letter. It does not indicate your agreement with the content of the letter. If you choose, you may submit a written rebuttal to me within 10 business days of this conference.

When All Else Fails … Moving to Non-Renewal

With a firm grasp on a teacher's overall performance and progress made on the plan of improvement, the principal is in a solid position to determine whether the teacher has made sufficient progress to stay, to have a modified plan of improvement follow into the next year, or to move toward non-renewal. In addition to looking at artifacts and evidence for improvement, some additional steps should be taken before having a conversation in which non-renewal might be a possibility.

- *Assemble evidence* from all sources, including the areas examined earlier in Chapter 6 (Improvement Planning) and Chapter 2 (Teacher Evaluation).
- *Seek input* from building-level leaders and others who have been working with the teacher. Care must be taken to collect only facts that can be substantiated with data, through artifacts, or in summaries that have been shared with the teacher.
- *Seek counsel* from the central office. Often the human resource person as well as the principal, superintendent, and others will meet with legal counsel to review artifacts, evidence, and data surrounding a teacher who is at risk for a notice of non-renewal. Generally, the principal will need to submit all documentation, including artifacts and evidence, in advance of this type of meeting.
- *Examine system-wide timelines, processes, and procedures* to ensure all documentation, processes, procedures, and messages at the site match the expectations of the system. Non-renewal and/or termination are fraught with legal issues (see Chapter 7).

Epilogue: The Case of Mr. Jansky

The plan of improvement and the letter summarizing the areas of concern with Mr. Jansky's performance in the classroom direct all efforts for improvement. In January 2015, Mr. Jansky and Mr. Forbes met to discuss the totality of the plan of improvement and Mr. Jansky's progress toward remediating identified deficiencies. Essentially, Mr. Forbes shared that not enough progress had been made in a manner that supported student learning; therefore, there would be movement toward non-renewal. The following summary was provided:

1   *Routines and rituals will be established, communicated, and implemented.*

   Unsatisfactory progress is being made. Students are still being sent into the hallways, sarcastic remarks are prevalent, and classroom disturbances are not handled consistently according to the written routines and rituals that were developed to fortify efforts.

2   *Lesson plans submitted every Monday morning will follow the district pacing guide.*

   Unsatisfactory progress is being made. Lesson plans have been habitually submitted late every week. Lesson plans do not follow the Algebra I content guide, and the state standards are not apparent.

3   *Classroom instruction will clearly adhere to the weekly lesson plan submitted, and necessary modifications will be explained to the department chair.*

   Unsatisfactory progress is being made. You have not submitted any assessments since November, grade-book entries stopped in December, and the midterm exam grades were displayed as X.

It is imperative that you address all of these concerns as they continue to be part of your improvement plan. Please sign and return this letter to me. Your signature does not indicate agreement with the content of the letter but only that you received it.

_____

(Signature)   (Date)

Potential Fallout

On a system level, a teacher who is going to be non-renewed will not be a happy camper in your building. In practice, the underperforming teacher will enlist the sympathetic ear of fellow teachers and, even if colleagues in the building know the teacher is underperforming, the others will listen, they will talk, and they will form judgments, maybe even take sides. A non-renewal decision can polarize teachers and staff. A non-renewal or a potential dismissal will become the focal point of many discussions in the faculty lounge, with union representatives, and with others, including central office leaders. If a situation is not handled well, it then reflects poorly not only on the marginal teacher but also on the administration. The best way to prepare for the potential fallout is to remember one fundamental concept: Issues related to personnel are off limits for discussion. The best thing that you can do is to listen and gently remind teachers, parents, and others that matters of personnel are confidential.

If a leader is new to the building, then anxiety levels might rise with the question, Who is next? Teachers will know the leader by the interactions he or she has with teachers, the types of conversations that permeate the building, and the fair ways in which teacher evaluation, professional development, and other supports are provided for teachers.

Final perspectives on working with underperforming teachers are offered in Chapter 10.

References

Bridges, E. M. (1990). *Managing the incompetent teacher* (2nd ed.). Eugene, OR: ERIC.

Center for Union Facts. (n.d.). *Teacher union exposed: Protecting bad teachers*. Washington, D.C.: Author. Retrieved from http://teachersunionexposed.com/protecting.cfm

Eltman, F. (2008, June 30). Firing tenured teachers isn't just difficult, it costs you. *USA Today*. Retrieved from http://usatoday30.usatoday.com/news/education/2008-06-30-teacher-tenure-costs_N.htm

Fullan, M. (2002). The change leader. *Educational Leadership, 59*(8), 16–21. Retrieved from http://www.ascd.org/publications/educational-leadership/may02/vol59/num08/The-Change-Leader.aspx

Harris, M. (2014, January 27). Deasy tells court: Teacher dismissal can cost district 'millions.' *Los Angeles School Report*. Retrieved from http://laschoolreport.com/deasy-tells-court-teacher-dismissal-can-cost-district-millions

Jackson, R. (2008). *The instructional leader's guide to strategic conversations with teachers*. Washington, D.C.: Mindsteps Inc.

Kaye, E. B. (2004). Turning the tide on marginal teaching. *Journal of Curriculum and Supervision, 19*(3), 234–258. Retrieved from http://www.ascd.org/publications/jcs/archived-issues.aspx

Lawrence, C. E., Vachon, M. K., Leake, D. O., & Leake, B. H. (2005). *The marginal teacher: A step-by-step guide to fair procedures for identification and dismissal* (3rd ed.). Thousand Oaks, CA: Corwin.

Maulding, W., & Joachim, P. (2000). When quality really counts. *Contemporary Education, 71*(4), 16–19. Retrieved from http://connection.ebscohost.com/c/articles/4786963/when-quality-really-counts

Nolan, J., & Hoover, L. A. (2011). *Teacher supervision and evaluation: Theory into practice* (3rd ed.). Hoboken, NJ: John Wiley & Sons.

Tucker, P. D. (1997). Lake Wobegon: Where all teachers are competent (or, have we come to terms with the problem of incompetent teachers?). *Journal of Personnel Evaluation in Education, 11*(2), 103–126. doi: 10.1023/A:1007962302463

Weisberg, D., Sexton, S., Mulhern, J., & Keeling, D. (2009). *The widget effect: Our national failure to acknowledge and act on differences in teacher effectiveness*. Brooklyn, NY: The New Teacher Project. Retrieved from http://carnegie.org/fileadmin/Media/Publications/widget.pdf

10 Final Perspectives

The sentiments of Weber (2010) continue to resonate with me: "[T]he fate of our country won't be decided on a battlefield, it will be determined in a classroom" (cover page). This explains why the topic of effective teaching must be an enduring conversation within and across schools and systems. It is through this conversation that leaders and teachers can make sense of instructional and classroom practices and the impact these have on student learning. Teacher underperformance, regardless of its degree, is detrimental to students and their long-term academic program. Leaders must act courageously in the best interest of students, because leaders have been entrusted to run a school where students must be afforded the very best instruction that can be delivered by competent teachers. An underperforming teacher can no longer be welcomed as a "butt on the bench" waiting to be traded off in NFL-like fashion. Make no mistake: Confronting underperformance and being ready to throw down the gauntlet to do what's best for the school community is not easy, but you can do it; no, you *must* do it!

There are many takeaways from this book that can support both the school leaders in having the difficult conversations related to teacher performance and, within the scope of this book, the teachers who are underperforming. In short order, this book has examined strategies to support teachers who struggle, to cue the leader on some strategies to engage in conversations, to frame plans of improvement, and then to make the tough decision that underperformance can no longer be tolerated. In no particular order, here are some takeaways to consider as you frame your next steps in working with underperforming teachers.

1   A lesson to remember: It's all about students. As the lead learner, students and teachers need you to be a "visible presence" through involvement in the instructional program.

2   A second lesson to remember: It's all about teachers and the investment leaders make in helping them to develop across the career continuum. Teaching matters; Schumacher, Grigsby, and Vesey (2011) remind us that teachers are "the single most important determinant of student achievement… and the common denominator in school improvement and student success" (p. 2) and, moreover, "effective teachers have a lasting positive impact on students; ineffective teachers can have a lasting negative impact" (p. 2). Generally, an underperforming teacher sits on a fence between the world of improvement and the world of business as usual. The leader's response to underperformance influences whether teachers move toward improvement, regardless of their level of performance.

3   Teacher evaluation is a multifaceted process that includes not only classroom observations but also engagement in other practices that can support teaching. These supports would include engaging in conversations about student work exemplars and participating as an active learner alongside teachers, for example. It's not fair explaining the importance of the topic, introducing the guest speaker, and then ducking out to your office to return phone calls.

4   In the *Wizard of Oz*, the cowardly lion wanted only courage. Diamond (2011) tells us that "*courage* is a kind of strength, power or resolve to meet a scary circumstance head on. Courage is called upon whenever we confront a difficult, frightening, painful or disturbing situation" (para. 5, emphasis in the original). As the lead learner and in a steady manner, you must confront underperformance. Think of the consequences for students and the school's instructional program if you do not act with due diligence. A leader who hides in the office letting underperformance continue will have a difficult time justifying to students and parents why no action was taken. Moreover, ask yourself, "Will I be able to look at myself in the mirror before I go to sleep?"

5   Accountability is not going away; however, teacher evaluation is more than accountability. Teacher evaluation is about making a commitment to teachers. Teachers need to know that you are there supporting efforts in the classroom and that, if they fall, you will swiftly be there to help lift them up, supporting improvement in whatever way makes sense.

6   "Gotcha games" are no longer what evaluation is about. Teacher evaluation is about processes that include timely feedback offered in a transparent manner.

7   Teacher effectiveness needs to be the centerpiece of all conversations. In fact, conversations about teaching and learning and the deliberate effort to improve these should be the norm and should direct leader attention and efforts.

8   Teaching and learning today are, in many ways, very different from what they were when we were classroom teachers. Leaders must be at the forefront learning and leading about such notions as personalized learning environments, digital tools that support teaching and student learning, and the utility of what the digital world can do to support learning in very purposeful ways.

To take creative license with the Black Eyed Peas song Boom Boom Pow (2009), "we are almost already 2000 late," in that digital platforms and software are now using analytics that allow teachers to monitor progress through real-time data that reflects student growth. We know that considerable research and literature exists about how teachers use student work to plan for instruction, use the work to discover where students need more attention and, through collaboration, engage in conversations about instruction, assessment, and other related topics (Zepeda, 2015). To keep up, leaders must be able to wisely champion how we remain engaged with the digital world because this is the world of today; tomorrow is too late.

9   Teacher evaluation systems have changed dramatically to the extent that teachers are now being evaluated on a host of items historically not part of an evaluation system. Student achievement, the results of surveys from parents and students, and such other items as classroom observations have entered the picture. Think creatively and resourcefully about how you and your school can capitalize on the types of rich data that can be examined in tandem to put focus on the instructional program and to examine their relationship to what teachers are doing in their classrooms. School districts can make a difference by not allowing the system to lose its mission-critical focus—teaching and learning. Think back to Chapter 3 and the Commitments to High Student Performance that the stakeholders in the Clarke County School District have made to step up their game.

10 In the final analysis, teacher performance rests on the shoulders of the principal. However, the principal does not own the problem of underperformance. At the building and system levels, personnel could begin to address teacher quality in various ways including "limit[ing] the number of rookie teachers hired to work in high-poverty and high-minority schools or ensur[ing] that beginning teachers come from programs or

institutions with a proven track record of supplying teachers who are much more effective than average" (Haycock & Hanushek, 2010, p. 51).

11 Beyond hiring, the site can provide numerous supports for underperforming teachers. To promote teacher leadership, master teachers can mentor, engage in peer coaching, and offer emotional support to underperforming teachers. The key is for building leaders to promote an ethos of care and concern for all teachers, even the ones who are struggling, who may be facing non-renewal, but who want to check back into their professional obligation to teach children in a way that signals upward trends in the classroom.

In summary, leadership really does matter when it comes to teacher effectiveness and student learning. I hope the contents of this book have been helpful in your efforts to ensure that effective teachers are the new norm in your building.

References

Black Eyed Peas. (2009). Boom Boom Pow. On *The E.N.D.* [CD]. Limoges, FR: Interscope Records.

Diamond, S. A. (2011, April 28). What is courage? Lessons from the cowardly lion: Tapping into your inner hero. *Psychology Today* online edition. Retrieved from https://www.psychologytoday.com/blog/evil-deeds/201104/what-is-courage-lessons-the-cowardly-lion

Haycock, K., & Hanushek, E. A. (2010). An effective teacher in every classroom. *Education Next*, *10*(3), 46–52. Retrieved from http://hanushek.stanford.edu/publications/teacher-quality

Schumacher, G., Grigsby, B., & Vesey, W. (2011). Development of research-based protocol aligned to predict high levels of teaching quality. *International Journal of Educational Leadership Preparation*, *6*(4), 1–9. Retrieved from http://files.eric.ed.gov/fulltext/EJ974343.pdf

Weber, K. (Ed.). (2010). *Waiting for "Superman": How we can save America's failing public schools*. New York: Public Affairs.

Zepeda, S. J. (2015). *Job-embedded professional development: Support, collaboration, and learning in schools*. New York: Routledge.

Index